Examining
The Seven Kings

A Study of Team Antichrist

Jason Lee Willis

Lura Publications

Mapleton, MN

Lura Publications
803 Silver Street E.
Mapleton, MN 56065
www.lurapublications.wixsite.com/books
williswrites.com

Book Layout © 2017 BookDesignTemplates.com

Examining the Seven Kings/ Jason Lee Willis. -- 1st ed.
ISBN 979-8-9903790-4-6

Dedication to Duane Guertin, my grandfather.
You died before I got to know you, but you left behind a book
about the End Times that later piqued my curiosity. I look
forward to discussing theories with you one day.

Contents

A DIFFERENT KIND OF CHRISTIAN

I don't like to be wrong, but if truth be told, I'm a bit of a coward, which is why I won't argue with my wife unless I know *for certain* that I'm right. This gives the impression that I'm "always right" when in fact I'm an anxious mess most of the time, but when I believe something to be true, hey, I'll go on record.

But the End Times?

Oh boy, why do I even bother tackling a book on the End Times when most of it's going to be wrong? Yes, I have an opinion, but so does every other Tom, Dick, and Harry. Why should I even bother?

Guilt?

If I don't say something, I'll feel worse than if I'm right.

I'm not smart. One look at my college transcripts, ACT results, G.P.A., or my results on Jeopardy could tell you this much. When I tried to figure out what to do with my life, I ended up as an English teacher because interpreting poetry, short stories, and plays came pretty easy to me. For the past three decades, that's what I did—interpret literature. As an English teacher, it was acceptable to be a little eccentric.

At the tail end of my teaching career, I began to reflect on my third grade teacher, who tried to put me into a special education program, which was weird because I could read at an adult level and would skip my homework assignments to work on preparing my slides for my new electric microscope at home. HOW DARE SHE! Yet after thirty years of sitting in special education meetings, I began to realize something about myself that my third grade teacher likely noticed too. So I asked my colleague, who was just completing her special education degree, and without explaining my purpose, she professionally agreed that I fit the top 20 identifiers for autism. Back in the 1970s, I doubt much was known about autism, and having worked with dozens of autistic students over the past thirty years, our shared traits became pretty obvious.

When I go down a rabbit hole, I go all the way down. Fortunately, my autistic wiring is pretty functional in social situations, which is why I was able to just "act the part" of a normal kid, but my thought process and obsession with random details made my literary interpretations quite different from most others.

With Biblical interpretations, it's the same way. I'm a terrier once I get hold of something, and I can't let go if I know there's a verse about something that amplifies the meaning.

So it's not intelligence or a degree that makes me worthy of your time—I'm just different.

I'm not trying to get attention by being weird for the sake of weirdness, but my brain often doesn't see things the same way a regular person sees it. So when I'd be in Bible studies, and the leader would throw out a theory, the whole group would nod in orthodoxy—and I'd be flinching.

"Yes, Jason?"

"What about…"

I'm not smart, but…if you compare my brain to a computer, a computer has processing speed, hard drive space, and ram. Now, my processing speed is garbage. If you catch me off guard, I can't solve problems under pressure. Two days later, I'll get what you want. I also have issues with my hard drive. I'm one of those "finger snappers" that can't quite pull up the information, but I know it's in there somewhere. But RAM? Ram is what allows you to have twenty programs or tabs open at once. My brain can see the big picture and the common themes between twenty unrelated things. That's my gift (I guess).

When I was on a playground, kids would say, "you're different" and it hurt a little. Granted, I didn't want to be like them, but I also didn't understand them either. Now, folks in my Bible studies say, "you're different" and suddenly it's a compliment.

I only bring up my wiring because of what happened in the days of Jesus. These folks had waited for centuries upon centuries for the prophecies to be fulfilled. Have you seen the number of prophecies in the Old Testament? Well, what happened? Jesus showed up…and… nobody put two and two together. All of those trained Pharisees got the interpretations wrong. Heck, even his disciples missed most of it.

The End Times will likely be the same.

We're going to be surprised.

Folks are going to be tricked.

The "orthodox" interpretations are going to be wrong.

If I was Tim LaHaye or Jerry Jenkins (loved those books), I'd be smiling all the way to the bank, but due to the popularity, I'd worry that all my theories were wrong—too many folks now believe them.

So a lifetime of being on the wrong side of normal has given me the confidence to be weird. Granted, I don't think I'm being weird. I think it's pretty black and white. This entire project is based on a couple verses that sparked an idea in my odd brain, so before you go and share this with normal people, keep in mind where I'm coming from.

Ready for the big idea?

The Antichrist will be genetically engineered.

He'll be a clone of sorts.

Before the weird finish, I'll be diving into some pretty traditional End Times verses as I build a twelve chapter argument (remember my RAM capacity) before I start tying the threads together.

CHAPTER ONE

BEASTLY BEHAVIOR

The Biggest, Baddest Bully

Picture that playground bully. Do they want your lunch money? Or do they want that *thing* you have? Is your bully filled with hatred and just wants to steal your joy? Whether you did something to antagonize that bully or you were in the wrong place at the wrong time, bullies have the capacity to just ruin your world.

King Nebuchadnezzar was an EPIC bully. He was a rich, powerful killer that didn't mess around. When the Jews crossed him, he wiped out most of the country, and then destroyed their most precious thing—the Temple of Solomon.

That's mean.

Here's where it gets horrible. The Jews got the tar beat out of them by their bully, but after the beating, the bully wasn't done. Imagine your playground bully punching you, breaking your favorite toy, and then forcing you to come home with him. Yep, Chad (um…) Nebuchadnezzar took bullying to a whole new level when he took his victims home with him so he could, you know, put 'em in their place.

'Chad'—an irredeemable bully.

(at first glance)

But there's something far stranger beneath the surface. Nebuchadnezzar went to sleep one night, feeling properly evil, only to be put into his place. Take Gargamel from the kid's show Smurfs. Gargamel is a proper villain, right? But imagine him suddenly having a nightmare about Walter White from Breaking Bad, where he sees Heisenberg murdering his enemies with poison, shivs, and explosions. A proper VILLAIN!

So when Nebuchadnezzar wakes from his own nightmare, the greatest villain to ever exist reveals the true meaning of eeeevillll (raised pinky). Chad…meet the Antichrist! Later in this book, we'll come back to what Chad saw, but there was another (John) who also happened to have a vision of the Antichrist.

Meanwhile on Patmos

John certainly read the book of **Daniel**, he absolutely heard Jesus give a different "End Times" talk right before his Crucifixion, and by the year 95 AD, John could've read all the other Biblical references to the End Times.

So he was fairly familiar with the prophecies before his sand castle was destroyed by that angelic foot on Patmos. The angel that visited him downloaded a lot of content that this book will not get into. In those opening chapters, it gives him symbolic messages for the seven churches and then jumps right into the

Seven Seals. After the Seven Seals, the information pivots to talk of the Two Witnesses (Check out *EXAMINING THE BE-LOVED DISCIPLE*) before John takes a short lunch break.

And then Revelation 12 gets dropped on his lap. To keep it short, I believe this chapter helps explain the backstory of Satan and the "War" between "Light and Dark" that is about to be discussed. Remember, much of the prophecies in chapters 1-12 have been about what happens to humans, but after 12, it gets a little more cosmic in nature. John is shown the backstory so that he understands the second half of the prophecy.

(cue the Darth Vader music)

> **[John 13:1] And I stood upon the sand of the sea, and saw a beast rise up out of the sea, having seven heads and ten horns, and upon his horns ten crowns, and upon his heads the name of blasphemy. [2] And the beast which I saw was like unto a leopard, and his feet were as the feet of a bear, and his mouth as the mouth of a lion: and the dragon gave him his power, and his seat, and great authority.**

Beast from Sea! That's all we get for a moniker. In fact, the term ANTICHRIST isn't used in the Book of Revelation. Yet this is who/what we're talking about. Buried in all the visuals, we'll get our details about him.

7 heads?

10 horns with 10 crowns?

Blasphemous name?

Animal symbolism?

Dragon? Oh, I know that one! That one is Satan! But the other stuff? Hmm....

[13:3] And I saw one of his heads as it were wounded to death; and his deadly wound was healed: and all the world wondered after the beast. [4] And they worshipped the dragon which gave power unto the beast: and they worshipped the beast, saying, Who is like unto the beast? who is able to make war with him?

Wounded head?
Healing?
Worship?
What impresses them so much?

[13:5] And there was given unto him a mouth speaking great things and blasphemies; and power was given unto him to continue forty and two months. [6] And he opened his mouth in blasphemy against God, to blaspheme his name, and his tabernacle, and them that dwell in heaven. [7] And it was given unto him to make war with the saints, and to overcome them: and power was given him over all kindreds, and tongues, and nations. [8] And all that dwell upon the earth shall worship him, whose names are not written in the book of life of the Lamb slain from the foundation of the world. [9] If any man have an ear, let him hear. [10] He that leadeth into captivity shall go into captivity: he that killeth with the sword must be killed with the sword. Here is the patience and the faith of the saints.

42 months? Why so specific?
How do you blaspheme God? How is this different from other villains?
More worship?
Kill by the sword? It's going to get rough!
(Cue Breaking Bad Theme Song)

[13:11] And I beheld another beast coming up out of the earth; and he had two horns like a lamb, and he spake as a dragon. [12] And he exerciseth all the power of the first beast before him, and causeth the earth and them which dwell therein to worship the first beast, whose deadly wound was healed.

Wait! There's more? Yep, the Beast from Earth is a different monster altogether, and we'll save a whole chapter for him. This "beast" seems to be a bit more "supernatural" since he's the one who "heals" Mr. Sea. Mr. Earth seems almost like a wizard:

[13:13] And he doeth great wonders, so that he maketh fire come down from heaven on the earth in the sight of men, [14] And deceiveth them that dwell on the earth by the means of those miracles which he had power to do in the sight of the beast; saying to them that dwell on the earth, that they should make an image to the beast, which had the wound by a sword, and did live.[15] And he had power to give life unto the image of the beast, that the image of the beast should both speak, and cause that as many as would not worship the image of the beast should be killed.

Notice the miracles? How will we be duped?
Image? Like a Captain Kirk mask?
Whatever it is, folks will be impressed!

[13:16] And he causeth all, both small and great, rich and poor, free and bond, to receive a mark in their right hand, or in their foreheads: [17] And that no man might buy or sell, save he that had the mark, or the name of the beast, or the number of his name. [18] Here is wisdom. Let him that hath understanding count the number of the beast: for it is the number of a man; and his number is Six hundred threescore and six.

This one gets people really worked up, which is why I'm going to skip it for this book. Do I have theories? Yep! Do I have enough confidence to argue them? (nope). But it can't be as obvious as the Arabic numbers 666, right? Didn't John use Roman numerals?

Characteristics Recap

So from just this passage, we can learn all sorts of information about Mr. Sea (the Antichrist) and Mr. Earth (his prophet).

World Leader: To do the stuff described, Mr. Sea will need to be a world leader. We've had plenty of tyrants, despots, and dictators, but Mr. Sea appears to have global outreach.

42 Months: One of the disciples asked Jesus when the world was ending (got a shrug). Daniel once asked when the world was going to end (another shrug). However, using improved Google Search terms, ask "After the Great Day of Tribulation, how much time will be left until the end of the world?" and you'll get it down to the day! Seriously. (Let there be no more delay). When the Antichrist officially takes power, he only gets a limited time. 42 months? That's just three and a half years.

Get the God Guys: Remember how America reacted to Pearl Harbor? 9/11? Something is going to happen around Seal 6 that will make the world rally behind their new leader (Mr. Sea). Christians are going to take the blame! They will need to be removed so that the rebuild can happen. This is the Brave New World purge.

Team Antichrist: From Barcodes to implanted chips, there are a million options for how to imagine the 666 prophecy, but at its heart, Mr. Sea will be controlling commerce (No Tickee, No Washee).

The 10: These are the puppet masters behind the scenes that will throw their support behind Mr. Sea. Remember, the world only learns about them at the very, very end, even though they might be around today. The lack of details mean this one can get interpreted in a variety of ways, so I'll mostly ignore this one even though I could toss out a dozen theories.

Immortality: Why does anyone fear God? While we certainly want "more life," the fear of God often comes with our fear of consequence (um, Hell). What if Mr. Sea could give you immortality without any consequence? Who'd need God then? He becomes his own Exhibit A. Folks knew him when. But he died. And THEN CAME BACK!!! We have no visual evidence of Jesus doing this, but apparently, Mr. Sea will be able to convince the whole world of his miracle. Tricky, tricky.

Wingman: While Mr. Sea (the Antichrist) is both Exhibit A and also the leader, it is Mr. Earth (the prophet) that does all the dirty work. He works his magic. He plots. He executes (pun intended). He tricks. Yet he is uniquely different from Mr. Sea.

Hates Babylon: This is another big topic that I'll skip for this book—the meaning of Babylon. While there is a little good in Babylon, she's mostly awful. Yet in the cosmic fight of good versus evil, Mr. Sea HATES Babylon. The enemy of my enemy is my friend? Not quite so sure with Babylon.

Seven Heads: All of these characteristics involve those last 42 months, but I believe the Seven Heads part of the prophecy tries to explain where the Antichrist is going to come from. Hidden in this prophecy will be the key to how Mr. Earth will trick the whole planet into worshiping Mr. Sea. Most of this book will be dedicated to understanding this single part of the prophecy, which luckily for us, is flat out explained by an angel.

The Prophecy Explained.

We have to skip ahead several chapters (don't you love cliff-hangers) before we get around to our explanation. I'll include all the references to Babylon (important, but not for this book) since the Seven Heads prophecy is snuck in there.

> **[John 17:1] And there came one of the seven angels which had the seven vials, and talked with me, saying unto me, Come hither; I will shew unto thee the judgment of the great whore that sitteth upon many waters:**
> **[2] With whom the kings of the earth have committed fornication, and the inhabitants of the earth have been made drunk with the wine of her fornication.**

Kings of the Earth? Like 10 of them?

> **[3] So he carried me away in the spirit into the wilderness: and I saw a woman sit upon a scarlet coloured beast, full of names of blasphemy, having seven heads and ten horns.**
> **[4] And the woman was arrayed in purple and scarlet color, and decked with gold and precious stones and pearls, having a golden cup in her hand full of abominations and filthiness of her fornication:**
> **[5] And upon her forehead was a name written, MYSTERY, BABYLON THE GREAT, THE MOTHER OF HARLOTS AND ABOMINATIONS OF THE EARTH.**
> **[6] And I saw the woman drunken with the blood of the saints, and with the blood of the martyrs of Jesus: and when I saw her, I wondered with great admiration.**

(focus on the Seven Heads)

[7] And the angel said unto me, Wherefore didst thou marvel? I will tell thee the mystery of the woman, and of the beast that carrieth her, which hath the seven heads and ten horns.

[8] The beast that thou sawest was, and is not; and shall ascend out of the bottomless pit, and go into perdition: and they that dwell on the earth shall wonder, whose names were not written in the book of life from the foundation of the world, when they behold the beast that was, and is not, and yet is.

[9] And here is the mind which hath wisdom. The seven heads are seven mountains, on which the woman sitteth.

[10] And there are seven kings: five are fallen, and one is, and the other is not yet come; and when he cometh, he must continue a short space.

[11] And the beast that was, and is not, even he is the eighth, and is of the seven, and goeth into perdition.

Was? Is not? Shall? Past and future? Yet dead?

More wonder and awe regarding Mr. Sea?

Not written? Hmm? An abomination?

Wisdom? Ooh, let my autistic brain try.

Heads=Mountains=Kings=huh?

5 have fallen=dead.

One is=alive

Is not yet come=future to John in 95 AD.

A traditional interpretation of that passage focuses on trying to understand Babylon, which is probably important. A couple of decades ago, folks were freaking out about Babylon and Iraq because of the man with the sinister mustache, Sadaam Hussein. Yes, Babylon's ruins are in modern day Iraq. Other folks freak out about the "seven hills" passage. Why? Well, the city of Rome is built on seven hills (kinda), and where is the Catholic Church based? Babylon=Catholic Church? Um, if I wanted to, I suppose I could stretch that theory to fit. I've encountered other theories that America is a modern day Babylon, but as fun as it is to compare Hecate and the Statue of Liberty, this theory takes a lot of elasticity.

I encountered an eccentric theory about the seven mountains aligning with the seven chakra mountains in a rebirth of paganism. I'm using that one for a novel series cuz it's got some really good geography (but not a lot of tangible support for Babylon). I've read theories that get so watered down that Babylon is represented by modern Christianity in its apostasy.

So if you don't mind, I'm skipping Babylon theories in this book.

Now here is where it gets tricky: The "eighth" is "of the seven." If you have the wisdom to understand the seven, then you'll certainly understand the eighth, who is the Beast of the Sea, or more commonly, the Antichrist.

So let's focus on that part of the prophecy.

Synonyms and Antichrists

Folks already have preconceived notions about the Antichrist. To sum them all up, he'll hate Israel (big list of candidates), is likely a Russian businessman who works at the UN to promote his private business, ties his left shoe laces first, and will name his cat Bubastis. That guy!

Or it's anyone who claims to be Jesus.

Or an Islamic messiah.

Or a Jewish messiah.

Perhaps all of the above.

Do you see what I mean about trying to "call" this stuff like it's the next play in a football game? "I told you they'd run the draw play!!!" Eventually, the coach will run a draw play and you'll look like Nostradamus. So looking back at the seven who create the eighth (the Antichrist) seemed to be a bit more tangible way of getting a scoop.

I've come to realize that modern Christianity likes meme-level simplicity.

"Satan—it's all his fault."

Yet the evil pantheon described seems to be anything but simple.

Now granted, I like complexity, so I'm not a fan of lumping everything together to "Satanify" wickedness. Do you remember Jesus describing "A House Divided"? Jesus name-dropped both Satan and Beelzebub to make a point about birds of a feather stickin' together.

Even in the last chapters of Revelation, the bad guys are:

A. Apollyon.

B. Beast from Earth

C. Beast from (C what I did there?)

D. Death

E. Hades (that one didn't work).

See what I mean about complexity? Throw in Satan (the Devil/Lucifer) and it gets even more complicated. But let's focus on the names for the Antichrist. In a nutshell, here are some of the commonly used phrases:

Son of Perdition

Antichrist

Man of Sin

The Abomination of Desolation

Title 1-Son of a #@*%$

There was a fascinating word (for me) found in Revelation 17:11 (and it's not the Bill Clinton definition of IS). The word is PERDITION:

[Rev 17:11] And the beast that was, and is not, even he is the eighth, and is of the seven, and goeth into perdition.

The word PERDITION basically means 'destruction, ruin, loss, and eternal ruin." Fun word, but it's been used in several other contexts, which piqued my curiosity and sent me down a very dark rabbit hole. Here is an overview of my underlined occurrences of PERDITION:

1 Tim 6: Perdition=destruction

Philippians 1:28:Token of PERDITION

Philippians 3:19 End is PERDITION

1 Cor. 1:18 Way to PERDITION

2 Cor. 4:3 Way to PERDITION

2 Peter 2:1, 2:3, 3:7 PERDITION of ungodly men

Heb 10:39 Into PERDITION

John 17:12 The son of PERDITION

Now, it was the last passage where the bottom of the rabbit hole dropped out for me. Until that passage, I was doing okay with the definition matching up with the modern curse of "You can go to (PERDITION)." It's a bad place. Very clear. The Greek word is APOLLYMI, which is very close to another name used, Apollyon. Not clear. It can be a noun or a verb. No problem with that either. But look at how John/Jesus used it:

[John 17:12] While I was with them in the world, I kept them in thy name: those that thou gavest me I have kept, and none of them is lost, but the son of perdition; that the scripture might be fulfilled.

As an English teacher, I'm used to personification, but the way Jesus used the phrase is alarming on multiple levels. First, this is a cool fulfillment of Psalm 41. Second, this passage has that "predestination" and "free will" conundrum. On one hand, Jesus flexes when he says he's lost "none of them" in reference to the disciples that God gave him, which leans toward the "free will" side of things (IE he could have lost them but didn't). On the other hand, Jesus brings up JUDAS (who'd just left the room) and says that Judas was NEVER his to lose since he was "the son of perdition."

Dang! What is this all about?

Again, it's not in my nature to "Satanify" everything evil into one basket. Remember, Satan is NOT the last enemy to be destroyed in the End Times. Heck, he once was an angel, remember? (Ask Ezekiel). Who personified evil before Satan "fell"? Perhaps the only way to understand John is to use another verse from John.

[John 1:1] In the beginning was the Word, and the Word was with God, and the Word was God. [2] The same was in the beginning with God. [3] All things were made by him; and without him was not anything made that was made. [4] In him was life; and the life was the light of men. [5] And the light shineth in darkness; and the DARKNESS comprehended it not.

More personification! Granted, this is a pretty cool passage about the eternal nature of Christ, but snuck in there is the opposite of light…the DARKNESS. Christ brought life into the universe, and the opposite of that is death, destruction, the DARKNESS.

Could Perdition=Darkness?

Being a "Son of Darkness" explains why the soul of Judas is different than any of the other disciples. His soul was never struggling with good and evil. It was evil from inception. His "father" was Perdition.

So does the Darkness have a name?

Perhaps it does.

If the LIGHT is Jesus, then the DARK is…(if only we had a verse that followed parallel structure like this). Oh wait, we do!

[2 Corinthians 6:14] Be ye not unequally yoked together with unbelievers: for what fellowship hath righteousness with unrighteousness? and what communion hath LIGHT with DARKNESS? [15] And what concord hath CHRIST with BELIAL? or what part hath he that believeth with an infidel?

So as Paul tried to make a parallel argument, he equates Darkness to a proper name, Belial. See what I mean about this rabbit hole?

Belial is a deep, dark, nasty hole, but I believe it explains a lot. There are a couple dozen Old Testament references to Belial, and just like Perdition, it can be used in a variety of ways. Many modern translations just remove it as a proper name so there are no complicated questions being asked. Belial is bad. "Satanified." Most often the English words for Belial (or Beliar) get changed to rebel or worthless. Remember, Satan was once an angel. What did he do? He Beliared. He rebelled. Belial is the spirit of rebellion.

So if the sins of the father are passed down from generation to generation, those who turn to Belial (like Satan) become the children of Belial, or even, the sons of Belial.

Since this is a book dealing with the End Times, remember that Satan is NOT the last enemy. The final two enemies of Jesus are DEATH and HADES. So when I read it, this is how I see it:

Death=Perdition=Belial (evil personified)

Hades=Beelzebub (both are underworld gatekeepers)

Here be Dragons

Okay, I got a little off track with that last section, but later on, I'll be trying to explain how being a "son of Perdition/Belial" might matter in the end. Mr. Sea and Mr. Earth have their roots in this big family tree of evil. Before I get into the other three "titles" for the Antichrist, let's deal with the dragon in the room.

Are dragons reptiles? Sure.

Are serpents reptiles? Yes.

Do biologists observe dragons today? No.

Does lore suggest dragons breath fire? Yes.

Does Leviathan breath fire? Yes.

Does the Leviathan have wings? Yes.

Do angels have wings? Yes.

Do angels have multi-faces? Yes.

Do dragons have multi-faces? Yes.

Was Satan once an angel? Yes.

Are there water dragons described in the Bible? Yes.

Could dragons be crocodiles?

(The Leviathan is NOT a crocodile!)

Could the snake in the Garden of Eden be a dragon?

Why not?

Throughout the Old Testament, dragons represent forces of chaos (Belial) in our world. From Rahab to Leviathan, there seem to be a number of them. Did God deal with them in the early days? After the fall? During the flood? Not exactly clear, is it?

Most cultures on the planet earth incorporate dragons, with most of them representing the forces of chaos. Multi-headed dragons were common symbols from Greek Mythology to Mesopotamian legends.

When John is shown the Red Dragon who tries to kill the Woman and Child, he would have understood the symbolism of the Red Dragon representing Satan. Revelation 12 is a backstory, a retelling of the fall in order to explain the redemption. As the Word, Jesus is a good writer, after all. He understands character arcs even when dealing with bullies and villains.

But is the Beast the same as the Red Dragon?

While they all belong to the House of Darkness, I'd like to argue that Satan wants to delay his punishment for as long as he can. No criminal wants to go to the electric chair, right?

The two Beasts, however, have different motivations than the Red Dragon. Yes, the Antichrist is similar to Satan, which is why they both have seven heads, but Satan was once an angel of light. The Antichrist is not a child of Satan. He is a Son of Perdition. He wants death and destruction.

Title 2-The Antichrist

The Book of Revelation doesn't actually use the term "Antichrist," yet it is John who uses the term in his letters. As a concept, everything about the Beast is antithetical to what Jesus represents, so he's both opposite and against...anti. I wrote an entire book on John the Beloved Disciple, and it is my view that he wrote Revelation, then the letters, and finally, his Gospel.

I could be wrong.

Remember, he first encountered the "Antichrist" prophecy when he was just a kid hanging out with Jesus. Let's look at Matthew 24 3-5:

> **[Matthew 24:3] And as he sat upon the mount of Olives, the disciples came unto him privately, saying, Tell us, when shall these things be? and what shall be the sign of thy coming, and of the end of the world? [4] And Jesus answered and said unto them, Take heed that no man deceive you.**
> **[5] For many shall come in my name, saying, I am Christ; and shall deceive many. [6] And ye shall hear of wars and rumors of wars: see that ye be not troubled: for all these things must come to pass, but the end is not yet. [7] For nation shall rise against nation, and kingdom against kingdom: and there shall be famines, and pestilences, and earthquakes, in diverse places. [8] All these are the beginning of sorrows.**

So this passage gives us a few interesting details regarding the Antichrist. John asks WHEN the End Times will be, and for the most part, Jesus shrugs it off by saying A WHOLE BUNCH OF STUFF needs to happen before we get to THE END TIMES. He walks John through Seals One, Two, Three, and Four in this section, finishing by saying these things are the "Beginning" of the End Times.

What's the biggest clue?

Seal Six.

This other stuff…well…it's bad but not Seal Six bad.

Within this passage, however, Jesus throws in a unique nugget: multiple Christ-Claimers, which is another way of saying multiple Antichrists, isn't it? Many…is that two, three, several?

This leads to another John passage. Let's look at 1 John 2:18 to see what other insights can be learned.

[1 John 2:18] Little children, it is the last time: and as ye have heard that antichrist shall come, even now are there many antichrists; whereby we know that it is the last time. [19] They went out from us, but they were not of us; for if they had been of us, they would no doubt have continued with us: but they went out, that they might be made manifest that they were not all of us. [20] But ye have an unction from the Holy One, and ye know all things. [21] I have not written unto you because ye know not the truth, but because ye know it, and that no lie is of the truth. [22] Who is a liar but he that denieth that Jesus is the Christ? He is antichrist, that denieth the Father and the Son. [23] Whosoever denieth the Son, the same hath not the Father: (but) he that acknowledges the Son hath the Father also. [24] Let that therefore abide in you, which ye have heard from the beginning. If that which ye have heard from the beginning shall remain in you, ye also shall continue in the Son, and in the Father.

First, I love how this is now "Old" John, likely written in the second century AFTER he'd written the Book of Revelation. They are "little children" to this old man.

Next, I'm impressed by how heavily he leans into the Trinity. Jesus=God=Holy Spirit. You can't pick and choose. He's dealing with second century Gnosticism at this time, so that makes sense why he's being so specific.

Notice how he also defines the spirit of the Antichrist as "a liar" and a "denier" that Jesus is the only way to redemption with the father. Pretty clear.

I can certainly agree that John's being a bit grandiose in this section. After all, in this time period, Gnostics were dressed up like Christianity yet espousing opposite doctrines. It was a very confusing time for new converts. So talk of the Antichrist could certainly be dumbed down to mean fake Christians. I've no problem with this.

However…there it is: Many Antichrists. How many? What does this mean?

I also picked up on that "Son of Perdition" tone Jesus used when talking about Judas never being up for grabs because…PREDESTINED. In the same passage he brings up "Antichrist(s)" John claims they were "not of us." Now that could be they weren't from Galilee, or they weren't Jewish, or they simply weren't good. It's unclear, isn't it? The whole "made manifest" point seems to be that God created these folks to help get us from the Garden Era to the New Jerusalem Era (which is the ultimate goal and a good thing). He needs these "Sons of Perdition" to do their things to push the story closer and closer to the final chapter.

A bit later, John adds more to this "Antichrist" concept:

[1 John 4:3] And every spirit that confesseth not that Jesus Christ is come in the flesh is not of God: and this is that spirit

of antichrist, whereof ye have heard that it should come; and even now already is it in the world. [4] Ye are of God, little children, and have overcome them: because greater is he that is in you, than he that is in the world. [5] They are of the world: therefore speak they of the world, and the world heareth them.

Again, strong anti-Gnostic preaching going on here. But here's a question: does he mean the "spirit" is now in the world or "the Antichrist" is now in the world. Unless he's a 2,000 year old vampire Antichrist, most likely the spirit. Yet I love how John uses the plural word "THEM" when talking about how the LIGHT has overcome them. He finishes by saying the "Antichrists" that have been overcome are "of the world."

Beast of Earth?

John brings the same point up again in another letter. Check out:

[2 John 1:7] For many deceivers are entered into the world, who confess not that Jesus Christ is come in the flesh. This is a deceiver and an antichrist.

Again, John is dealing with the Gnostic heresy here, but in his arguments, he clearly establishes that there is not single a antichrist but "many" antichrists. How many could there be? That's a question now bouncing around in my brain.

Title 3-The Man of Sin

One of the best descriptions of the Antichrist can be found in Paul's second letter to the Thessalonians. Remember, that even though the Book of Revelation has not been written, Nebuchadnezzar freaked out about the Antichrist six centuries earlier. John heard more about it on the Mount of Olives.

[2nd Thessalonians 2:1] Now we beseech you, brethren, by the coming of our Lord Jesus Christ, and by our gathering together unto him, [2] That ye be not soon shaken in mind, or be troubled, neither by spirit, nor by word, nor by letter as from us, as that the day of Christ is at hand. [3] Let no man deceive you by any means: for that day shall not come, except there come a falling away first, and that man of sin be revealed, the son of perdition; [4] Who opposeth and exalteth himself above all that is called God, or that is worshiped; so that he as God sitteth in the temple of God, shewing himself that he is God. [5] Remember ye not, that, when I was yet with you, I told you these things? [6] And now ye know what withholdeth that he might be revealed in his time. [7] For the mystery of iniquity doth already work: only he who now letteth will let, until he be taken out of the way. [8] And then shall that Wicked be revealed, whom the Lord shall consume with the spirit of his mouth, and shall destroy with the brightness of his coming: [9] Even him, whose coming is after the working of Satan with all power and signs and lying wonders, [10] And with all deceivableness of unrighteousness in them that perish; because they received not the love of the truth, that they might be saved. [11] And for this cause God shall send them strong delusion, that they should believe a lie: [12] That they all might be damned who believed not the truth, but had pleasure in unrighteousness.

Lies, deception, signs, wonders…humanity is going to get tricked HARD. Paul echoes what John said and took it up a notch when he establishes that the Antichrist is not just going to be a deceiver but will also claim to be GOD. That's a human with a BIG ego. But we've seen this claimed before in history, haven't we?

Notice how Paul connects the phrase "man of sin" with "son of perdition." Verse 8 is often translated to the "lawless one" where here it only says wicked. Even though I could dumb this all down by saying "Antichrist is bad" these phrases help link to other areas of the Bible.

Title 4: The Abomination of Desolation.

The great bully Nebuchadnezzar dreamt of the Antichrist and the "things" leading up to his arrival on earth. In fact, Daniel added a whole bunch more (we'll have a chapter on Daniel) about the End Times and the Antichrist, including his big finish in Daniel 12:

> **[Daniel 12:11] And from the time that the daily sacrifice shall be taken away, and the abomination that maketh desolate set up, there shall be a thousand two hundred and ninety days. [12] Blessed is he that waiteth, and cometh to the thousand three hundred and five and thirty days. [13] But go thou thy way till the end be: for thou shalt rest, and stand in thy lot at the end of the days.**

Remember how Paul talked about the Man of Sin being "revealed in his time"? This section seems to echo the idea that the Antichrist will appear shortly before the Apocalypse. The phrase "Abomination of Desolation" is most commonly used and is found in several other spots, including a different prophecy from Daniel in chapter 9:

> **[Daniel 9:27] And he shall confirm the covenant with many for one week: and in the midst of the week he shall cause the**

sacrifice and the oblation to cease, and for the overspreading of abominations he shall make it desolate, even until the consummation, and that determined shall be poured upon the desolate.

Here's a big "jump to conclusions" mistake that folks made in the time of Jesus. It was a complicated prophecy, but getting an 80% is failure when Jesus is trying to warn you.

Did Nebuchadnezzar dream of the Antichrist(s)? Yes (1/1)

Are the four beasts described in Daniel related to the Antichrist(s)? Yes (2/2)

Does Antiochus Epiphanes have a connection to the Antichrist(s)? Yes (3/3)

Did Antiochus Epiphanes desecrate the temple and stop daily sacrifice? Yes (4/4)

Is Antiochus Epiphanes the Abomination of Desolation?

Apparently...not.

So much of the prophecy fit (and we'll come back to this, don't worry) that folks look at Antiochus Epiphanes and apply things to Head #8—THE ANTICHRIST that Chad worried about. But Jesus took a moment during his "End Times" talk on the Mount of Olives to clarify that the Abomination of Desolation prophecy mentioned in Daniel HAS NOT happened yet.

Matthew, Mark, and Luke all wrote this one down. John wrote the Book of Revelation, so...why waste ink? Here's Matthew 24:

[Matt 24:15] When ye therefore shall see the abomination of desolation, spoken of by Daniel the prophet, stand in the holy place, (whoso readeth, let him understand:) [16] Then let them which be in Judaea flee into the mountains: [17] Let him which is on the housetop not come down to take any thing out of his

house: [18] Neither let him which is in the field return back to take his clothes. [19] And woe unto them that are with child, and to them that give suck in those days! [20] But pray ye that your flight be not in the winter, neither on the sabbath day: [21] For then shall be great tribulation, such as was not since the beginning of the world to this time, no, nor ever shall be.

See…still to come! Jesus even gets a bit snarky with (whoso readeth, let him understand:)!!!

The world didn't come to an end 3 ½ years after Antiochus Epiphanes rode a pig through the Temple of Solomon because…that's not what the prophecy meant (apparently).

I'll get back to this point with a whole chapter on Antiochus Epiphanes and also a whole chapter on the "triggers" for the End Times, but for now, just know that this phrase "Abomination of Desolation" has some seriously dark tones to it.

CHAPTER TWO

AN ITCHY TRIGGER FINGER

Talking about the End Times can be a bit gloomy—the doom gloom. Many preachers would rather talk about duckies and bunnies, feelings and faith, lessons and learns. Non-Believers would rather plug their ears to any of it since the End Times is antithetical to humans improving because of evolution and shows the fragility of a planet billions of years old. Ending things in a snap (sorry Thanos fans) is a bit too epic and silly. Both sides tend to look at all the mayhem and destruction described in the End Times and think: why is God so mad?

So let's make a comparison.

Anyone who's ever raised a child understands the hot stove metaphor. Say it. Barricade it. Get angry about it. But that kid is bound and determined to touch the stove regardless of your efforts and warnings. As a loving parent, you do everything you can to explain the hurt and danger to the child since using the stove is a necessary part of life, but that child will eventually find a way to put that little hand on the hot, hurtful stove (or any other similar metaphor). In this metaphor, the parent acts like God. We love the child, so we find numerous ways to warn the child. Ultimately, the child does what the child must do. Regardless of parenting, the lesson will be learned. A bad parent does nothing and just lets it happen. A loving parent warns us.

So I've come to see the End Times prophecy as a love letter from God rather than an angry God looking to spank his child. Each little warning is that "all knowing" look from our parent. Whether the first lesson like the "hot stove" or much later lessons like the dangers of fraternities while at college, the End Times prophecies show us that God is with us on our journey of painful discoveries. At some point, God hopes you'll realize "Hey, you told me about this" and discover the love of the Creator. The End Times are intended for the habitual stove-touchers.

Since this book examines the Antichrist and Company, we're going to focus on some of those "trigger warnings" specifically involving the Antichrist in order to see what else can be gleaned.

The Apostasy

Apostasy is an interesting concept for Corporate Christianity to deal with. From Jesus telling his disciples to baptize all nations to the White Horse seal visualizing a conquering figure, it seems pretty obvious that the game plan was not just to save the chosen people (the Jews) but also to evangelize the whole world. Jesus essentially says that the End Times will not even happen unless this step comes first.

> **[Matthew 24:14] and this gospel of the kingdom shall be preached in all the world for witness unto all nations; and <u>then</u> shall the end come.**

and…then…

So go get them, kids.

Christianity went out into the world, and two thousand years later, there are churches all over the world. Granted, all that Christianity we threw onto the walls of the world didn't always stick, but hey, we went. We tried. We evangelized.

But before all the thunderbolts and lightning of the End Times, a trigger will be the end of this evangelizing effort. Using a tree metaphor, the seed of Christianity took root long ago, grew into the big tree, and then produced fruit. Right before the end, the fruit begins to rot.

That's the Apostasy.

Here is how Paul described it to Timothy.

> **[1 Tim 4:1] Now the Spirit speaketh expressly, that <u>in the latter times</u> some shall <u>depart from the faith</u>, giving heed to seducing spirits, and doctrines of devils; [2] Speaking lies in hypocrisy; having their conscience seared with a hot iron; [3] Forbidding to marry, and commanding to abstain from meats, which God hath created to be received with thanksgiving of them which believe and know the truth. [4] For every creature of God is good, and nothing to be refused, if it be received with thanksgiving: [5] For it is sanctified by the word of God and prayer."**

Do you see why Apostasy is seen as rotting fruit? The tree of Christianity, which provided so many good things, will stop providing nourishment. The Great Commission is over. Time to deal with the Evil Ones before pushing the reset button.

So the good news for Corporate Christianity is that there will be PLENTY of believers in the End Times, but the problem for them is that the mainstream MESSAGE being taught is WRONG. This has nothing to do with the vegans as much as the overall message. The CHURCH will be the problem.

The Church itself will be a trigger.

So before ANY preacher can point to a sign and say SEE, SEE, SEE, it means that we'll be neck deep in apostasy. God is going to pull the plug on Corporate Christianity not because of the pagans, heretics, and atheists but because of the Christians within.

God rarely blindsides his people. In literature, there's a concept called "Chekhov's Gun" which means you need to preview any prop prior to it being used in the story. Throughout the Bible, God follows this principle. The Apostasy is no exception. There are two key examples of moments where the MESSAGE has been corrupted on earth.

> **[Genesis 6:8] But Noah found grace in the eyes of the LORD. These are the generations of Noah: Noah was a just man and perfect in his generations, and Noah walked with God. [10] And Noah begat three sons, Shem, Ham, and Japheth. [11] The earth also was corrupt before God, and the earth was filled with violence. [12] And God looked upon the earth, and, behold, it was corrupt; for all flesh had corrupted his way upon the earth.**

The picking is pretty slim when only 8 folks are saved, and keep in mind, it only credits 1 of those 8 as being righteous. We know what happens later with Ham. There's another moment a thousand years later of rock bottom Apostasy.

> **[2nd Chronicles 34:1] <u>Josiah was eight</u> years old when he began to reign, and he reigned in Jerusalem one and thirty years. [2] And he <u>did that which was right</u> in the sight of the LORD, and walked in the ways of David his father, and declined neither to the right hand, nor to the left. [3] For in the eighth year of his reign, while he was yet young, he began to seek after the God of David his father: and in the twelfth year <u>he began to purge</u> Judah and Jerusalem from the high places, and the groves, and the carved images, and the molten images.**

So Josiah was just a kid. All of Israel had turned away from God, and some kid keeps the fires of faith lit. The story of Josiah takes an interesting turn once he halts idol worship and begins to seek to restore classic God worship.

> **[14] And when they brought out the money that was brought into the house of the LORD, Hilkiah the priest found <u>a book of the law</u> of the LORD given by Moses.**

Josiah's faith wasn't even Bible-based since they didn't HAVE the Bible. Then again, what did Noah have, right? When God looked out over his creation in these two instances, we were down to just two people. Like a cold fire, God found a single ember and relit the whole thing.

Did all the folks living down the block from Noah realize they were wicked?

How about the folks living in Jerusalem? Did they realize they'd switched teams?

The problem with Apostasy is that you're in the majority and the majority is wrong. Let's examine another Apostasy warning from Paul:

[2 Thess 2:3] Let no man deceive you by any means: for that day shall not come, except there come <u>a falling away first</u>, and that man of sin be revealed, the son of perdition;

Mr. Sea will be revealed. Before that happens, though, the "falling away" must happen first. The White Horse rode out into the world, and just as Jesus predicted on the Mount of Olives, none of the End Times things will happen until the Gospel is Preached to all Nations. Once that has happened, the APOSTASY must begin.

Rot.

This is why TRADITION became so important in worship. If we kept doing things the way grandma and grandma's grandma did things, it means we are holding the status quo. So when trying to make things CONTEMPORARY, we're trying to change that FIG growing on the tree. What's the only kind of change that can happen to a fully formed fig? Rot.

But God's holding our hand as this Apostasy happens because in our hearts, we know what's going to happen next.

The Man of Sin Revealed

The previous passage from 2nd Thessalonians not only brings up the Apostasy but also brings up an interesting concept. Following the Apostasy (which I interpret to be the White Horse era of evangelism), the countdown will begin when Mr. Sea is revealed. The Man of Sin, the Son of Perdition, the

ANTICHRIST will show up in our darkest hour to fool Corporate Christianity. (cue Bonnie Tyler) We'll need a hero. Mr. Sea will be our Knight in Shining Armor to help us through tough times.

Now, the tough times I speak of are an event foreshadowed throughout the Bible: the Great Day of Tribulation. Now, I could write a whole chapter just on this event, so I'll keep it brief so I can stay on our Beastly hero. The Sixth Seal (and other moments) describe a singular global disaster. It's likely something predictable. It will kill a LOT of people (sorry Lot. Hope you're not salty about the pun). I'd bet on a meteor strike. Whether you subscribe to a finger-snapping magical poof or a flesh sizzling pyroclastic cloud created by sudden impact, this is the RAPTURE moment too. Bye, bye, worthy Christians.

Once the dust literally settles, the world will need a hero to step up, and Mr. Sea will be ready for the challenge.

Strangely, both Daniel and the Fab-Four on the Mount of Olives (James, John, Andrew, Peter) were denied an answer for the question they asked: When will the End Times take place? Um…complicated? But ask how long it will be from the Sixth Seal OR Mr. Sea being revealed, you'll get a very, very, very specific answer:

> **[Daniel 12:11] And from the time that the daily sacrifice shall be taken away, and the abomination that maketh desolate set up, there shall be <u>a thousand two hundred and ninety days</u>. [12] Blessed is he that waiteth, and cometh to the <u>thousand three hundred and five and thirty days</u>.**

Recap: When Mr. Sea is revealed (the abomination…), we'll have EXACTLY 1,290 days left. Chew on that, Daniel!!! And how much time from the Great Day of Tribulation until the end? Considering these two things overlap, it appears to me that forty-five days after Alexander's Terrible, Horrible, No Good, Very Bad Day, the Antichrist will officially reveal himself.

And how will he reveal himself?

As I mentioned earlier, the popular interpretation of the Abomination of Desolation mentioned by Daniel is (according to Jesus) kinda wrong. The key parts of the prophecy include: a temple, a bad guy, and the daily sacrifice. All three items are symbolically open to interpretation. We'll get into this concept later. For now, we're just looking at it as a trigger. Let's see how Jesus said it:

> **[Mark 13: 14] But when ye shall see the <u>abomination of desolation</u>, spoken of by Daniel the prophet, <u>standing</u> where it ought not, (let him that readeth understand,) <u>then</u> let them that be in Judaea flee to the mountains**

Even though Jesus (winks) when he playfully suggests that folks have the interpretation wrong, this is nevertheless a TRIGGER for things going wrong. Notice how this one does mention AofD like a person, including a verb "standing" which really implied a singular man, but the curious part is the "where it ought not." Certainly, the popular interpretation is THE TEMPLE but since it's been torn down twice, perhaps we should keep our mind open. Regardless of the meaning (we'll go there fully next chapter), it means that once this villain does show up, it's time.

The Days of Noah Return

I brought up the Apostasy not just as a trigger warning, but also as something we need to use for comparison and understanding. Even though Josiah is a cool example of the whole ember to flame concept, I think Noah provides better insight. So does Peter:

[1 Peter 3:3] **Knowing this first, that there shall come in the last days scoffers, walking after their own lusts, [4] And saying, Where is the promise of his coming? for since the fathers fell asleep, all things continue as they were from the beginning of the creation. [5] For this they willingly are ignorant of, that by the word of God the heavens were of old, and the earth standing out of the water and in the water: [6] Whereby the world that then was, being overflowed with water, perished: [7] But the heavens and the earth, which are now, by the same word are kept in store, reserved unto fire against the day of judgment and perdition of ungodly men. [8] But, beloved, be not ignorant of this one thing, that one day is with the Lord as a thousand years, and a thousand years as one day. [9] The Lord is not slack concerning his promise, as some men count slackness; but is longsuffering to us-ward, not willing that any should perish, but that all should come to repentance. [10] But the day of the Lord will come as a thief in the night; in the which the heavens shall pass away with a great noise, and the elements shall melt with fervent heat, the earth also and the works that are therein shall be burned up. [11] Seeing then that all these things shall be dissolved, what manner of persons ought ye to be in all holy conversation and godliness, [12] Looking for and hasting unto the coming of the day of God, wherein the heavens being on fire shall be dissolved, and the elements shall melt with fervent heat? [13] Nevertheless**

we, according to his promise, <u>look for new heavens and a new</u> <u>earth</u>, wherein dwelleth righteousness.

Peter is so fascinating. Remember, he doesn't have the vision given to John in the Book of Revelation. Yet he seems to know the whole plan. He starts off by clearly stating that he's talking about the End Times. Next he brings up the Daniel Paradox about the End Times being both predictable and unpredictable. This makes him fixate on the "day" when everything will change with fire. This could be Armageddon or Seal Six. Finally, he shows a big picture understanding that the purpose of the "Fire" is to clean things up for a new heaven and earth, which the end of Revelations gives in detail.

In the middle of Peter's summary of the End Times prophecy, he clearly makes a connection to the flood. Not only does he make a simple metaphor (water=bad=fire) but he connects it to an old prophecy: the same word. If you've read my other works, you understand what I mean by "spurious texts." There's a prophecy mentioned in the Book of Enoch that happened before the flood. In it, it promises both fire and water. Peter is obviously referencing this text (even though we don't know which version of it=spurious).

So why connect the two disasters?

Let's go to Matthew for more insight.

[Matthew 24:36] But of that day and hour knoweth no man, no, not the angels of heaven, but my Father only. [37] But <u>as the</u> <u>days of Noah</u> were, so shall also the coming of the Son of man be. [38] For as in the days that were before the flood they were eating and drinking, marrying and giving in marriage, until the day that Noah entered into the ark, [39] And knew not until the flood came, and took them all away; <u>so shall also the</u>

coming of the Son of man be. [40] Then shall two be in the field; the one shall be taken, and the other left. [41] Two women shall be grinding at the mill; the one shall be taken, and the other left. [42] Watch therefore: for ye know not what hour your Lord doth come. [43] But know this, that if the goodman of the house had known in what watch the thief would come, he would have watched, and would not have suffered his house to be broken up. [44] Therefore be ye also ready: for in such an hour as ye think not the Son of man cometh.

The major point being made here goes back to the Daniel Paradox. Remember, Daniel asked "When is the End Times..." and was given a vague answer. Trying again, Daniel asked another way and learned that the End Times will last approximately 3 ½ years, depending on the trigger (Meteor or Mr. Sea). Jesus was asked the same question, and he deferred to God. He didn't say September 13, 1988, did he? He shrugged and claimed it'll be sudden.

Yet buried within this explanation is the same parallel to the flood. Jesus, not Peter (and not me), goes on record by drawing parallels between the flood and the fire.

Okay, Jesus, I'll look closer at the flood.

Before we look at the flood, I had a bit of a head scratcher. What made God cleanse the earth in the flood? Will it be the same reason he'll cleanse the earth with fire?

I want you to remember something: Josiah. From King Solomon to King Amon, Israel turned from God to worshiping false gods (nasty gods, too). Wars, violence, hedonism, child sacrifice...Holy Cow! (pun intended). And don't bother looking around the globe for better God people, either. They were just as bad. By the time Josiah showed up, Israel had been totally corrupted. Remember, they didn't go to church or even have a Bible. Yet THIS Apostasy didn't make God pull the plug, did it?

Heck, according to Eusebius, it sounds like the Christian Church was down to just a handful of believers thanks to the oppression of the Jews and Romans in the third century, yet God didn't pull the plug then either.

So now let's look at the world of Genesis. Chapter Five is a bunch of genealogy and Chapter Seven records the details of the Ark and Flood, so the only thing we have is Chapter Six:

[Genesis 6:1] And it came to pass, when men began to multiply on the face of theearth, and daughters were born unto them, [2] That the sons of God saw the daughters of men that they were fair; and they took them wives of all which they chose. [3] And the LORD said, My spirit shall not always strive with man, for that he also is flesh: yet his days shall be an hundred and twenty years. [4] There were giants in the earth in those days; and also after that, when the sons of God came in unto the daughters of men, and <u>they bare children</u> to them, the same became mighty men which were of old, men of renown. [5] And GOD saw that the <u>wickedness</u> of man was great in the earth, and that every imagination of the thoughts of his heart was only <u>evil continually</u>. [6] And it repented the LORD that he had made man on the earth, and it grieved him at his heart. [7] And the LORD said, I will destroy man whom I have created from the face of the earth; both man, and beast, and the creeping thing, and the fowls of the air; for it repenteth me that I have made them. [8] But Noah found grace in the eyes of the LORD. [9] These are the generations of Noah: Noah was a just man and perfect in his generations, and Noah walked with

God. [10] And Noah begat three sons, Shem, Ham, and Japheth. [11] The earth also was <u>corrupt</u> before God, and the earth was <u>filled with violence</u>. [12] And God looked upon the earth, and, behold, it was <u>corrupt</u>; for all <u>flesh had corrupted</u> his way upon the earth.

Baaad. The earth was so bad that God had no other choice than to destroy it. He didn't pull a Josiah and rekindle some embers of faith, did he? He didn't pick a Roman General, whip up a miracle at a bridge, and turn the oppressor (classic Saul<Paul) into a hero—and flip the tables like he did with the Roman Catholic Church. It was too baaad.

What made it so bad?

Violence?

Four thousand years after these little psychopaths, we created machine guns, landmines, B-52s, and nuclear bombs. There was a 50 year period where we had two world wars that took the lives of millions. According to archeologists, the folks in Genesis Six certainly didn't have pistols. So what kind of violence are we talking about? As much as the fantasy writer in me wants to picture dudes riding in a T-Rex cavalry, I struggle to see how violence is any different than it's been the past four thousand years.

Unless the shared trait is not violence...

Being wicked and evil is also mentioned. Tree worshippers then. Tree huggers now. Sexually immoral then. Sexxxually immoral now. Aside from a pretty intense Puritan era, we've had naked heathens walking around most of those 4,000 years. Even the 4,000 years of Israel, God's chosen people, has had much longer stretches of evil behavior than good behavior. Take an evil savage Hun and pit them against an evil Soy Boy from

Seattle. Seriously? No contest, right. Yet before the Flood, folks were evil continually. Wow! What was that all about? A world full of Jeffrey Dahmers? Now, Jeffrey Dahmers are famous because of being so uniquely evil. Folks aren't like that on my block, right?

What did these Pre-flood folks do that made God so disgusted? What will be the shared trait that brings upon the End Time fires?

The answer might still be right there.

Corrupt Flesh

Imagine God as a painter. He's staring at the blank canvas, and then day after day, he dabs his brush of creation into the primordial paint jar and presto! It is good.

Good. That's God's reaction to each day. Each phase of creation was His design, and it pleased him to see it. Each molecule. Each DNA twist and turn. It pleased Him.

Adam? Heck, Adam pleased God also. Depending on your interpretation of God's Omniscient ability to see what was going to happen, it also seems as if he created Adam with free will knowing that he (and humanity) needed to fall in order to become perfected in the end. Adam and Eve fell in a perfect world, and they might've been restored and saved in a perfect world until...HEY! STOP THAT! I SEE YOU! THAT'S WRONG YOU LITTLE WEIRDOS!

What am I talking about?

Genesis Six gets twisted into pretzels. As you can see from the 1611 King James Version, a longstanding interpretation is that

Fallen Angels (Sons of God) reproduced with women (Daughters of Man) and produced Giants (Nephilim).

Atheists giggle at this, which is why many newer interpretations shy away from the Old School interpretation. Pay no attention to the Giant behind the curtain, right?

Well, then you have to ignore a lot of the Bible.

Noah…giants in his life.

Abraham…giants in his life.

Moses…giants in his life.

King David…eliminated the giants in his life.

God does not like giants!!!

Why?

He didn't make them.

While I'm not sure of the physics of biology of Genesis Six, if an Angel and a woman did manage to produce a child, the DNA would be…MESSED UP! Giants are messed up humans. They're hybrid mutants. (just read all the passages and you'll see what I mean). Yet they are also spiritually different. Perhaps even soulless.

I've read some old lore from Ethiopia that believes a slain giant becomes a demon.

My point is that Genesis Six describes an ABOMINATION. Humans didn't make them. The Fallen Angels made them. Big difference from the violence and evil of the Hun Dynasty.

If the Ethiopians are right, humans couldn't even cleanse their world. If a grizzly bear hunts your village, you kill it. If a giant hunts your village, you kill it and get possessed! Wow, what a conundrum. It has the possibility of spreading like a virus, doesn't it? In the Ethiopian legends, Noah's flood is pretty similar except for the part where it describes God's archangels coming down to deal with the Fallen Angels and giants.

Think the Ethiopians are crazy?

Then what is Jude talking about here:

[Jude 6] And the angels which kept not their first estate, but left their own habitation, he hath reserved in everlasting chains under darkness unto the judgment of the great day.

Genesis Six is the strongest reference to the "Sons of God" being naughty.

Creating a new species was wrong. I believe this was the ABOMINATION that disgusted God.

The World Will Marvel

When the Man of Sin (the Antichrist...Mr. Sea) shows up, there's going to be something very, very special about him. He's going to do something no one has ever done before. Yes, there are references to a mortal wound being healed, but hey, Rasputin did that a century ago. No marvel in the "gasp...I'm dead...NOT!" routine.

Science, however, holds the potential to make the world marvel.

Genesis Six was another example of Chekhov's Gun. Our Heavenly Father uses the example of the Sons of God creating something they shouldn't create as the ULTIMATE NO NO. Don't touch the stove, kids, and whatever you do, don't be like the Sons of God and turn on the gas and blow up the whole house.

So let's talk about Daniel, DNA, and us.

CHAPTER THREE

DANIEL, DNA, AND ME

Before we get to Daniel, let's go back to one of my favorite verses involving the Antichrist given to us by John. Again, the vision given to John has a peculiar structure at times, and after introducing the Antichrist, suddenly, there's an "oh yeah" section where *more* explanation is given because John is a bit confused (like the reader):

> [John 17:7] And the angel said unto me, Wherefore didst thou marvel? I will tell thee the mystery of the woman, and of the beast that carrieth her, which hath the seven heads and ten horns. [8] The beast that thou sawest was, and is not; and shall ascend out of the bottomless pit, and go into perdition: and they that dwell on the earth shall wonder, whose names were not written in the book of life from the foundation of the world, when they behold the beast that was, and is not, and yet is. [9] And here is the mind which hath wisdom. The seven heads are seven mountains, on which the woman sitteth. [10] And there

are seven kings: five are fallen, and one is, and the other is not yet come; and when he cometh, he must continue a short space. [11] And the beast that was, and is not, even he is the eighth, and is of the seven, and goeth into perdition. [12] And the ten horns which thou sawest are ten kings, which have received no kingdom as yet; but receive power as kings one hour with the beast. [13] These have one mind, and shall give their power and strength unto the beast.

H=M=K and $5+1+1=7=8$.

Got it. This reminds me of when I'd have to explain grammar to clueless sophomores and I'd cruise up to the desk and claim, "Oh, this is easy!" Yet Chapter 17 is even worse because instead of just claiming it to be "easy" the angel says, "Oh, you gotta be smart to figure this one out."

Huh?

The first condition explained by the angel is that the Antichrist has connections to the past, present, and future. This is explained four times. Was. Is. Shall. Past. Present. Future.

Next, the symbolism key is explained. Seven heads? They represent seven mountains? But the seven mountains also represent seven kings. Kings. Seven. Got it?

Then repeat it back to me:

The Antichrist will have a connection to seven kings.

Which kings?

Well, John is alive in the year 95 (or so) when he gets this prophecy, and the angel is pretty specific when he says: 5 kings have already died prior to this=was. One of the kings is currently living during your life=is. The seventh king will come later (likely close to the end)=not yet come.

Most of the remaining chapters in this book will try to figure out candidates for these seven heads=seven kings. It'll be fun. Yet in the previous chapter, I tried to explain what made the Antichrist such an ABOMINATION. My theory about the "giants" being an abomination since they were "unnatural" tried to connect to the flood/fire prophecy. If there's any truth to this theory, is there any set up for it in scripture?

I think I see it.

Of the Seven

How do you explain genetics to somebody born before the 20th Century? For most of human history, we've never been able to look within a human to see the complex structure known as DNA. Even today, many American kids fail this test in science class. In chapter 17, the Angel rolls up his sleeves to explain it to John: "Confused, John? This is easy! The Antichrist is a genetic hybrid using samples of the previous antichrists to make up an 8th being."

Of the seven!

The phrasing of the Antichrist being "of the seven" is strange also. Why is it worded so weirdly? English translations have struggled with it. Look at popular ways they wrote it:

KJV/Aramaic/ASV/Berean/Websters/NET/WorldEnglish /

ESV/D-R: of the seven

Young's Literal/LSV: Out of the Seven

NIV/ESV/NRSV/Majority/HCS/CSB/: belongs to the seven

NAB: really belongs to the seven

Good News/Contemporary/Amplified: one of the seven

New Living: Like the other seven

The tame/lame interpretation of this is that there'll be some sort of "connection" between the seven kings from history and the 8th antichrist, who'll be the biggest baddy of all time. A connection like… "Ooh, they're all eeevillll."

A slightly more ambitious interpretation of this passage is that there could be a family tree connection that puts all of these "sons of Perdition" into one big family tree. That's not bad. In fact, I really like that theory (but for the Prophet). Simply making the Antichrist the great-great-grandchild of some awful person doesn't rip the fabric of existence and upset God's view of his creation. Yes, it also involves genetics, but that "Perdition Gene" is carried through thousands of generations with only 8 occurrences of it manifesting into something awful. That certainly doesn't seem like a trigger worthy of being labeled an ABOMINATION.

The world will marvel!!!!!!!!

A family tree? Check out the Jesus lineage. Even bad guys and girls had their part in the Jesus family tree.

Cloning? Game changer. Everybody knows scientists like Dr. Frankenstein have been on the precipice of replicating life for the last few centuries. For the past fifty years, pop culture has slowly made us aware of this ability with movies like Jurassic Park as a cautionary tale.

What if we threw caution to the wind? What if there were no moral parameters for genetic engineers?

Could we clone someone?

I'll save all of this speculation for the end of this book. Let's see if the Book of Daniel goes into concepts resembling cloning.

Daniel Dumbed Down

Like the Book of Revelation, Daniel is about as complex as it gets. Because of this complexity, you can twist and shape it into about anything you need. Unlike Revelation, which was dropped in John's lap during a single day at the beach, Daniel contains several segments from several different time periods. It is not a single, cohesive prophecy. With this caveat in mind, here is my dumbed down summary of Daniel:

Chapter 1: A little background on Daniel himself

Chapter 2: Nebuchadnezzar's Antichrist dream

Chapter 3: The Golden Image Incident

Chapter 4: Nebuchadnezzar's Mental Breakdown Incident

Chapter 5: Belshazzar's Writing on the Wall Incident

Chapter 6: Daniel in the Lions' Den Incident

Chapter 7: Daniel's Beastly Dream of the Future

Chapter 8: Daniel's Dream of the Future

Chapter 9: Daniel's Dream of the Future

Chapter 10: Daniel's Dream of the Future

Chapter 11: Daniel's Dream of the Future

Chapter 12: Daniel's End Times Dream

As you can see, these 12 chapters jump between four different kings and cover a range of topics. Some of the chapters have no prophecies at all and just talk about stuff that happened to or around Daniel. Others are dreams of other people. It ends with Daniel's dreams of the future. Chapters 7-12 are problematic because it's tough to know specifically how far into the future they're talking. These chapters are easily twisted to mean anything you want them to mean. Jewish scholars would keep it historically BC. Christian scholars see it as both historical (now) and also prophetic. We're going to focus on Chapter 2 in this chapter and then later come back to Chapter 7 when searching for clues about the 7 kings.

Dreaming of the Antichrist

As I mentioned earlier in this book, I find it fascinating that King-"Chad"-the-bully dreams of an even bigger bully. Nebuchadnezzar is so troubled by what he dreams that it brings Daniel into his life. Yet it wasn't Daniel's dream…it was Chad's dream. Ponder that for a bit. What purpose did it serve? Is it the equivalent of not letting your child watch a Rated-R movie? God didn't want Daniel to dream it? Too much for him?

Regardless, Nebuchadnezzar is given what Daniel refers to as "the deep and secret things" from God. He is shown the future. And it troubles him! So he tried to get SOMEBODY to explain this nightmare to him. Before Daniel is brought in for the explanation, Arioch declares to King Chad:

> **[Daniel 2:28] But there is a God in heaven that revealeth secrets, and maketh known to the king Nebuchadnezzar what shall be in the latter days.**

So this prophecy is very specific. We're talking about the latter days…the End Times.

Rrrr you ready kids?

[Daniel 2:31] Thou, O king, sawest, and behold a great image. This great image, whose brightness was excellent, stood before thee; and the form thereof was terrible. [32] This image's head was of fine gold, his breast and his arms of silver, his belly and his thighs of brass, [33] His legs of iron, his feet part of iron and part of clay. [34] Thou sawest till that a stone was cut out without hands, which smote the image upon his feet that were of iron and clay, and brake them to pieces. [35] Then was the iron, the clay, the brass, the silver, and the gold, broken to pieces together, and became like the chaff of the summer threshingfloors; and the wind carried them away, that no place was found for them: and the stone that smote the image became a great mountain, and filled the whole earth. [36] This is the dream; and we will tell the interpretation thereof before the king. [37] Thou, O king, art a king of kings: for the God of heaven hath given thee a kingdom, power, and strength, and glory. [38] And wheresoever the children of men dwell, the beasts of the field and the fowls of the heaven hath he given into thine hand, and hath made thee ruler over them all. Thou art this head of gold. [39] And after thee shall arise another kingdom inferior to thee, and another third kingdom of brass, which shall bear rule over all the earth. [40] And the fourth kingdom shall be strong as iron: forasmuch as iron breaketh in pieces and subdueth all things: and as iron that breaketh all these, shall it break in pieces and bruise. [41] And whereas thou sawest the feet and toes, part of potters' clay, and part of iron, the kingdom shall be divided; but there shall be in it of the strength of the iron, forasmuch as thou sawest the iron mixed with miry clay. [42] And as the toes of the feet were part of iron, and part of clay, so the kingdom shall be partly strong, and partly broken. [43] And whereas thou sawest iron mixed with miry clay, they shall mingle themselves with the seed of men: but they shall not cleave one to another, even as iron is

not mixed with clay. [44] And in the days of these kings shall the God of heaven set up a kingdom, which shall never be destroyed: and the kingdom shall not be left to other people, but it shall break in pieces and consume all these kingdoms, and it shall stand forever. [45] Forasmuch as thou sawest that the stone was cut out of the mountain without hands, and that it brake in pieces the iron, the brass, the clay, the silver, and the gold; the great God hath made known to the king what shall come to pass hereafter: and the dream is certain, and the interpretation thereof sure.

So if I'm Daniel, where do I begin? There's a ton of information to explain in this passage. King Chad is freaking out. So…I'll give him the most surface level explanation.

Me: this monster you dreamed of is the Antichrist. He's not going to be here for a long, long time. But don't worry, God will "smote" him.

King Chad: why did he look so funny?

Me: The different parts are to show you the passage of time. Beginning with you (the gold head), there's going to be several different kingdoms that will pass. You and me? We'll be long gone by then. But cheer up! God's going to "smote" him and set up his own Kingdom that'll be described in Chapter 21 of Revelation.

King Chad: Huh?

Me: Oh, sorry. Jumped ahead a bit there. Never mind.

King Chad: So this dream and bad guy is all about the End Times approximately 2,600 years from now?

Me: Give or take a few decades because of the Gregorian calendar.

King Chad: Huh?

Me: Oh, sorry. Never mind. Yes, a long time from now.

King Chad: So I'm the golden head, which represents the present. The other parts of the scary dude represent the future. I think I got it. Since Babylon represents an evil empire that's harsh on the Jews, does this mean there will be other kingdoms coming that will also be harsh on the Jews?

Me: I think you're onto something there.

King Chad: Cool. If I'm the golden head, can I stop this prophecy from coming true by just building a great big golden statue that looks like me? No iron. No bronze. No clay. Just 100% me!

Me: Are you jumping ahead to Chapter 3?

King Chad: Maybe…

Me: Can we focus on only Chapter 2. I wanted to explain my theories on DNA to my readers. I'm ending this imaginary monologue now. Goodbye, King Chad.

The Seed of Men

Is King Chad nuts?

Nope. Daniel says the opposite when he says Nebuchadnezzar has tapped into some of the deep and secret things of God about the End Times. In other words, this prophecy matters. This prophecy is predicting something very, very, very important. As we've already discussed, the Antichrist has many names and is mentioned in several spots of the Bible. Since his arrival is a trigger for the clock to count down the destruction of the world, he matters!!!

Let's widen the lens a bit and look at what was shown in the dream.

The Antichrist is made up of a bunch of different parts, isn't he? Ignoring the symbolism of the types of composition, this being is made up OF others. Of. Yes, it seems to be more of a linear timeline than John's Chapter 17, but the visual...this is Dr. Frankenstein's monster. We're going to slap together different body parts to create this monster.

Obviously, when you're making a human, you wouldn't use gold, iron, brass, or clay, would you? These construction materials can make swords, candle holders, or assorted coffee cups, but a human? To make a human, you'd need...oh, there it is.

Seed.

Ew.

I'm not sure what sort of science classes were required of sophomores back in 538 BC, but most sophomore boys have discovered the basic biological workings of...seed. I'm not certain of the symbolism of iron or miry clay, but I do understand why this vision involves seed. In order to make a human, you're going to need a little...seed.

Ew.

Between Mary Shelley's Frankenstein and Dolly the Sheep, science didn't just discover DNA but mapped it out to discover it was made up of 23 chromosome pairings with 6.4 BILLION (apply pinky to lips) letters in the code.

That's complicated.

In the dark ages of the 1980s, I have to admit being a bit disappointed to learn that scientists couldn't just whip up something in a blender and pour it out. As an aspiring Biotechnology major, my future consisted of flipping around a few of those 6.4 billion letters to create a mutant soybean. Starting from scratch…that's kinda hard. Tinkering? Much easier.

So it makes sense that Chad's Monster is glued together with the "seed of men" with bits and pieces from others to create this singular, unique creation.

ABOMINATION

We've already looked at Daniel's "Abomination of Desolation" trigger, but Daniel 12:11 is not the only time he mentions such a thing. Many historians think Daniel is garbage because its prophecies were so accurate.

(Sigh.)

Their problem is that the visions came true. Babylon<Persia<Greece. In two different prophecies, Daniel called it. He saw Alexander the Great hundreds of years before he showed up. That's good stuff. Because it was so accurate, scoffers believed the Book of Daniel was a poetic way of writing down the history after it happened.

(Sigh.)

But if it really was written before 538 BC…Double Dang! Not only did Alexander the Great come true exactly as Daniel predicted, but that means the other stuff was likely going to happen also. This is why End Times scholars like this book. Not only did it predict Alexander but it also predicted another bad guy—Antiochus Epiphanes. This is the main villain in the Maccabees saga. While we'll save him for another chapter, he did a bunch of the stuff written in Daniel.

Even though he had connections to the "Abomination of Desolation" trigger and even did some bad stuff to the temple (another trigger), Jesus set his disciples straight when he referenced this prophecy as something that has NOT YET happened.

With my 5+1+1=7=8 theory, paying attention to Antiochus Epiphanes is important, but the ABOMINATION is still waiting to happen. Yes, Antiochus Epiphanes was eeevilll, and yes, he did wreck the temple and bring worship to an end, but this was NOT THE TRIGGER for the End Times. The world did not end 3 ½ years later. Forget about the earthly Solomon's Temple (which gets destroyed all the time). Both TEMPLE and ABOMINATION need to be reimagined. Antiochus Epiphanes is introduced like this:

> **[Daniel 8:9] And out of one of them came forth a little horn, which waxed exceeding great, toward the south, and toward the east, and toward the pleasant land. [10] And it waxed great, even to the host of heaven; and it cast down some of the host and of the stars to the ground, and stamped upon them. [11] Yea, he magnified himself even to the prince of the host, and by him the daily sacrifice was taken away, and the place of his sanctuary was cast down.**

We'll come back with a whole chapter on AE, but scholars are pretty unanimous that this is a clear reference to AE, and this is the first of several other references to the Abomination of Desolation that culminates with Jesus speaking to his disciples with the caveat (let the reader understand). In other words, this is a challenging thing to understand.

It's even hard to say.

The term "Abomination of Desolation" can be written in several different ways depending on your translation. The concept can range from "riding a pig" to genetic cloning. Since I'm arguing for an EPIC understanding, I'm going to ignore pig riding and Solomon's Temple as options. With the nebulous "Sons of Perdition" reference mentioned earlier, let's look closer at the meaning of the phrase used.

Siqquc Shomen

If Jesus had said, "Watch out! When you see "Siqquc Shomen" standing where it shouldn't be, the End Times clock will start," you'd wonder: Who? What? English translators have struggled to give a clear understanding.

Basically, the phrase translates to "Abomination of Desolation." Clear? Dig deeper and the explanation is that Siqquc is anything "that pertains to idolatrous worship" and Shomen is "a concrete form of "that maketh desolation." This could be anything eeevilll.

Yet, the background on this term dates back much older than Daniel. Apparently, the term Siqquc Shomen comes from an older phrase that means "Baal of Heaven" which was written as "Baal Shamayim."

(Quick recap: Baal was the storm god of the Canaanites. Bad stuff. The Hebrews of Exodus and even Pharaoh, who named his daughter after Baal's sister Anath, had worship addiction issues with the Golden Cow God. Joshua had major issues with Baal worshippers too. Baal=bad.)

My point?

If the 7 Heads are not connected by a big family tree, then what connects them?

Their religion?

Bringing up Antiochus Epiphanes gives me something else to ponder beside the genetic Frankenstein concept. This is how the Book of Maccabees 1:43 describes the situation:

> **[41] Moreover king Antiochus wrote to his whole kingdom, that all should be one people, 42 And every one should leave his laws: so all the heathen agreed according to the commandment of the king. 43 Yea, many also of the Israelites consented to his religion, and sacrificed unto idols, and profaned the Sabbath.**

His religion? The term Siqquc Shomen gives us a clue. What was Antiochus Epiphanes' religion? Worshiping Siqquc Shomen instead of God. So when we investigate the candidates for the Seven Kings, we'll use this "dark side of the force" idea as a condition.

Back to the Beasts

So now that I've introduced you to the concepts behind the Antichrist(s), we'll do a deep dive into the past to meet some of our candidates. We'll get back to my DNA theory again, but I wanted to end with my formula for dividing up the candidates.

As established by the Book of Revelation, the 5+1+1=7=8 theory spells out that 5 Kings came before the year 95 AD (over thousands of years), 1 of them was alive in 95 AD (quite easy), 1 will come after 95 AD (that's 2,000 years of choices), and the Antichrist will come in the final years of the End Times.

7 vs. 4?

Since Daniel and Nebuchadnezzar both dreamed of the Antichrist and "beasts," the key to narrowing things down might be found in those pages. Remember, Daniel is writing approximately 600 years BC. While it was possible that all 7 Kings were still in his future...nope...there are not seven mentioned....just four.

Four?

Obviously, numerous prophecies in Daniel pointed to Alexander the Great. It also seems pretty clear that Antiochus Epiphanes is called out. That leaves two. Mr. 95 AD and Mr. 2K future. Four.

What happened to the other three?

My theory is that those 3 came BEFORE Daniel.

Nobody dreams about them or their kingdoms or their...mountains...because they've already lived and died. King Chad certainly dreams of Mr. Potato Head #8 (the Antichrist) as well as some major historical plot points, but nobody dreams backwards to the past.

So our search will be defined by:

- Someone born prior to 600 BC.
- Someone who worshiped Siqquc Shomen
- Any connection to Perdition talk
- And someone who God foreshadows with a shout-out.

Why a shout-out?

Heck, the King of Easter Island coulda been one of he most vile humans to ever walk the earth, but it isn't in God's style to NOT warn us. He loves the "I told you so" hot kitchen stove lessons, doesn't he?

CHAPTER FOUR

THE LOIN OF THE BEAST

When I was growing up in South Dakota, I had a recurring nightmare. It stemmed from the fact that I went from a brand new house in the city of Sioux Falls to an old farmhouse out in the country. This old farmhouse had a root cellar instead of a cement basement. It didn't even have stairs. To access the basement, you'd have to go outside and open up the heavy door, which revealed a staircase covered in webs.

Creepy.

The dirt floor smelled...old.

And the stone foundation that mirrored the rooms above it had a peculiar feature: a hole. This broken or unfinished wall was right out of Edgar Allen Poe's "Cask of Amontillado." As a child, I'd peer into the darkness and expect a vampire or mummy to come crawling out.

So it fueled my nightmare.

The nightmare manifested itself into my belief that some immortal, undead creature lived in my basement, and that the builders of the house had somehow unearthed it from his slumber.

Have you ever read my fiction series?

Since this is a grown-up Bible study, and I likely lost credulity by brining up a DNA Frankenstein Antichrist, I'm not going to get into all the fun stuff I found down in the rabbit hole, but…there was significant stories about ancient kings, and many of those obvious secret society organizations connect to ancient symbolism about an ancient, beheaded king.

So when it comes to dead kings from antiquity, I have quite a bit of imagination.

Let's roll up our sleeves and take a look.

Surprisingly, we don't have a huge list of villains to evaluate. Granted, the timeline is a pretty narrow 4 millennia of choices since we don't hear/care about anything other than Middle East history. Beyond that, we're looking for a reference in the Bible. So here's the list I quickly came up with:

Name: Context: **Evil traits: Eliminating Factor:**

Cain1st Murderer, Not a king?

LamechMurder/PolygamyKing?

HamMean, 1 of 8 saved on the Ark

NimrodIncest/Magic…!!!

Abraham's PharaohHorny, Found a place for them. Kind?

ChedorlaomerWarrior King, An ally of Abram?

EsauHungry, Not a king?

Joseph's PharaohSupports Slavery, Saves Israel

Infanticide PharaohPost-Term Abortion…

Moses's PharaohHard Heart!…!!!

AmalekBloodlicking, Not human?
Baalam/BalakDefeated soundly
Anak/OgBeing Big, Not human?
GoliathBeing Big, Not human?
Not a King?
King Agag????
King of TyreSatan Possessed?...
Ben-Hadad of Syria????
Sennacherib of AssyriaNorthern TribesDefeated
Pharaoh Necho of EgyptAmbitious??
and...NebuchadnezzarJudea, Repented!

Did I miss somebody? Who knows? These guys are what I'm left to deal with. Remember, I'm searching for the top three "sons of perdition" candidates, and while being evil is important, I'm also looking for willfully the enemy of God.

Cain, for example, is notorious for being the first murderer, but that was because of jealousy. He still made sacrifices to God. Esau, likewise, is a bad brother but nowhere near an evil despot. Plus...not kings.

When I looked at all of these names, the most obviously wicked "king" would have been a Pharaoh from Exodus. Now, killing infants is a terrible policy, but I chose the "hard-hearted" pharaoh since he willfully rejected God and the Egyptian Gods in favor of his secret worship of Anath and Baal. His priests also defied God with their own snake trick. He'll be Chapter 6.

With a little research, I learned that the "Tower of Babel" guy not only had a funny name—Nimrod—but also had a ton of legends and lore about his wickedness. When you realize the purpose for building the tower, his wickedness became more obvious than Ramses and the Great. He'll be Chapter 5.

So what about Chapter 4?

If I were forced to rank a third king, I might've been rushed to include Sennacherib or Nebuchadnezzar because of what they did to Israel. I also might've picked one of those guys associated with "giants" because of how much God despises those abominations. A significant thought entered my mind: The End Times will be like the Days of Noah! Thus, if those days were so bad, perhaps I should look closer at the early days.

Initially, I was a bit disappointed by the "lack" of details. Here's a brief summary of the pre flood world:

Genesis 1: Days of Creation

Genesis 2: Life in the Garden

Genesis 3: The Fall

Genesis 4: Cain and Abel, Cain stuff

Genesis 5: The Descendants of Adam

Genesis 6: Wickedness, Nephilim, Building the Ark

Genesis 7: The Flood

Genesis 8: The New World

See? Not much there. However, I believe I found the story within Genesis. Right after Cain murdered Abel, and he went to the Land of Nod, there is a time-lapse. While we can't be certain how much time passes between Day 6 and the "Fall," it's equally challenging to imagine the timeline of Cain and Abel. We do get the lifespans in Genesis 5 to match, but we don't get much of an answer for where Cain's wife comes from or why he needed a mark if there were only 2-3 people on earth. Speculate those answers!

Yet hiding in Genesis 4 are some curious moments. Big picture: Genesis is a summary given to Moses from God while hanging out in the fiery tent during the Exodus. It'd been almost a thousand years since the flood (according to the Genesis timeline), and God selected only the most important details to give the Hebrews.

So why did God bring up Lamech?

Ah…a clue!

Let's take a closer look at Cain first:

4:10 And (the LORD) said, What hast thou done? the voice of thy brother's blood crieth unto me from the ground. 11 And now art thou cursed from the earth, which hath opened her mouth to receive thy brother's blood from thy hand; 12 When thou tillest the ground, it shall not henceforth yield unto thee her strength; a <u>fugitive and a vagabond</u> shalt thou be in the earth. 13 And Cain said unto the LORD, My punishment is greater than I can bear. 14 Behold, thou hast driven me out this day from the face of the earth; and from thy face shall I be hid; and I shall be a fugitive and a vagabond in the earth; and it shall come to pass, <u>that every one that findeth me shall slay me</u>. 15 And the LORD said unto him, Therefore whosoever slayeth Cain, vengeance shall be taken on him sevenfold. <u>And the LORD set a mark upon Cain</u>, lest <u>any</u> finding him should kill him. 16 And Cain went out from the presence of the LORD, and dwelt in <u>the land of Nod</u>, on the <u>east of Eden</u>.

Being a vagabond and fugitive seems to suggest that Cain could not find rest. He became a lone wolf. Strangely, his concern is that he'll get killed in retribution. BY WHOM??? Strange… He doesn't express worry about Mom and Dad. He mentions "EVERYONE" will hate him for this deed, and if they find him, they'll kill him in retribution. Huh? WHO? I guess if Moses didn't need more details, neither do we.

The Mark of Cain has received endless speculation, but in a nutshell, he gets a physical change. It is a visual identifier so that EVERYONE who encounters him can tell him apart. This isn't a SCARLET LETTER of shame, mind you. This is a "DON'T KILL THIS GUY" or "IT'LL BE WORSE FOR YOU" visual warning. Very strange. I've read theories about it being a racial mark all the way to it being the creation of werewolves. Gingers? The Mark of Cain. Africans? The Mark of Cain. Epilepsy? The Mark of Cain. Crooked Teeth? The Mark of Cain. Neanderthals? The Mark of Cain. Blonde hair and Blue Eyes? The Mark of Cain. The Mark is a speculative mess.

However…I find it interesting that WHATEVER God did to Cain, it also came with geographic isolation. He walked away from the Eden region and went to the land of wandering…Nod. Even if the Mark had nothing to do with genetic identity, a thousand years of genetic isolation would further separate the "appearance" of these two population groups.

So let's continue to follow the story of Cain:

> **4:17 And <u>Cain knew his wife</u>; and she conceived, and bare Enoch: and <u>he builded a</u> <u>city</u>, and called the name of the city, after the name of his son, Enoch. 18 And unto Enoch was born Irad: and Irad begat Mehujael: and Mehujael begat Methusael: and Methusael begat Lamech. 19 And Lamech took unto him <u>two wives</u>: the name of the one was Adah, and the name of the other Zillah. 20 And Adah bare Jabal: he was <u>the father of such</u> as dwell in tents, and of such as have cattle. 21 And his brother's name was Jubal: he was <u>the father of all such</u> as**

handle the harp and organ. 22 And Zillah, she also bare Tubalcain, an <u>instructer of every artificer in brass and iron</u>: and the sister of Tubalcain was <u>Naamah</u>.

23 And Lamech said unto his wives, Adah and Zillah, Hear my voice; ye wives of Lamech, hearken unto my speech: for I have <u>slain a man</u> to my wounding, and a <u>young man</u> to my hurt.

24 If Cain shall be avenged sevenfold, truly <u>Lamech seventy and sevenfold</u>.

Who was Mrs. Cain? Genesis doesn't explain. The Ethiopians (and other cultures) have names for the daughters of Adam, who were the mismatched twins of Cain and Abel. Speculation allows for Eve to give birth to a child on a yearly basis, and if she lived approximately the same lifespan as Adam, she holds the potential to give birth to hundreds of children from age 20 to 200. Sarah? Elizabeth? Eve has a perfect uterus and 900 year lifespan. Ponder that! So speculation allows that Cain could've wandered the earth for a century and came back to grab a wife from among 100 or more daughters of Eve. I'm going to drop this issue now.

A city? Ooh…that's interesting. In contrast to the peaceful agrarian Sethites, the Cainites live in fear, and when you live in fear, you need protection from scary things. So what scared them? Without clarification of reproductive habits, the speculative population boom could be impressive. Cain could have a thousand grandkids running around. Who knows? Obviously, you need at least a handful to qualify for a "city." There is also a paradox between the "wandering" Cain and the Cain who built a city. Is he like a long-distance trucker who goes out into the world for long stretches at a time? Who knows?

A few generations later, we get LAMECH. Now, there are only a few strange verses to study, but you have to ask yourself why did God even bother giving them to Moses? Why bring up Lamech? In the most literal interpretation, the flood wipes out EVERYBODY but 8 humans. Following Cain's exile, God could have ignored the rest. "And the Kennedys lived unhappily ever after." Yet God went out of his way to slow things down to remind those Hebrews all about Lamech. There MUST be a reason to do this when the lesson is so...strange.

So let's look at the clues from the text:

Characteristic A: A Frisky Fella

Boring stuff first. A few generations passed. Now remember, these generations are much, much, MUCH different than the generations of Moses, who maxed out his lifespan at 120 years. When aligning the pre flood generations, you have the POSSIBILITY that the generations overlapped each other. You'd live long enough to see your great-great-great grandchild. That's weird. Now, the heirs of Seth lived righteous lives, and they waited years past puberty to start having kids during the self control of their SECOND CENTURY of life!!! Assuming that Cain had no self-control, the descendants of CAIN are spreading like wildfire and would quickly OUTNUMBER the SETHites. So not only would they get started early but they could pop out a new child yearly. The city would be full and then some.

Along with the possibility of wild child production, notice that Cain is a polygamist.

Gasp.

Sorry, but…Abraham? Sarah, Hagar, Keturah…um. Moses! (Aaron and Miriam clear their throats): Zipporah and Tharbis (folks didn't know about her, did they?). King Solomon!!! (Do 300 concubines count?) Well, it lists 700 official wives.

I'm not trying to diminish marriage here, but the OT hadn't quite established this as a HUGE DEAL. Put on your tinfoil hat for Adam and you can see EVE, WOMAN, and even whispers of another named LILITH. Yes, bringing up a famous polygamist might've been used to shame Moses and the Hebrews into a traditional marriage system.

Lamech certainly could've had loose sexual morals, which accounted for him marrying Adah and Zillah. Perhaps there was a strong moral code that's not explicitly stated in Genesis. Cain chose incest while Seth chose…poof! A magically appearing non-relative. Why not? We just don't get the details. My point is that sexual immorality is not the make-or-break characteristic to separate sheep from goats. Abraham? Jacob? David? See what I mean?

What's in a Name?

Since we know so little about this time period, let's look a bit closer at the meaning behind the names to try to gain some clarity. The name LAMECH means "powerful." This leads me to think of the Conan the Barbarian type who becomes king because he is the biggest, baddest alpha male in the pack. There are also some variations of LAMECH that bring in a "low" connotation, which DOES have connections to the PERDITION concept. The word Perdition comes from the word apóleia/apóllymi, which means "cut off, destruction, severed."

The root also reminds me of Apollyon, the destroyer, and Belial, "the vile, worthless, never to rise" one. So the name Lamech has some wicked possibilities.

(SIDE NOTE: Twenty years ago, I found an article about this name. In it, the writer connected the old Hebrew to the term AMALEK (from Exodus). He proposed a Harry Potteresque "HE-WHO-MUST-NOT-BE-NAMED" cursed name. In this same crazy article, he mentioned that the local Arabians who worshiped AMALEK used the word MERAK also. Who's Merak? That is the "loin of the beast" in the BIG DIPPER constellation. How many stars? 7. What do the pole stars lead to? An 8th. I feverishly jotted this stuff down in my notebook, later used it for my novels, but now I can't find a trace of the article. It was cool, but you can't always trust what you read on the internet.)

Adah is far less nefarious. Her name means "ornament." She's pretty.

Zillah's name means "shadow." Huh? So many options here. Racially, it could mean a genetic separation has already begun (meh). Or...more fantastical...it could mean she is related to that Hebrew legend of Lilith and she's some witchy woman. Or...it could reflect her personality and she's the Gothy Stevie Nicks queen.

The boys: Jabal means leader/stream. Jubal means led/stream. Now Tubalcain for some reason kinda means the same thing: leader/leading. Yawn.

Naamah: Her name means "beautiful/pleasure" which is very "boom, chicka, wow wow" yet gives us little else. I'll tell you one thing, though, there are some myths and legends about her.

Just like it was ODD for Lamech to even get a mention, it's even ODDER that Naamah gets a reference. WHO CARES about the geography before the world flood? WHO CARES about a city destroyed by the world flood? Well, God felt it was important to mention her.

The legends and lore? Naamah was 1 of 4 women on the Ark. The Hebrew Midrash goes so far as to suggest that she was a singer and the WIFE OF NOAH!!! Now, I've found a dozen names for Noah's wife from a dozen mythologies. Yet Naamah shows up in several contexts involving the Ark. Curious. It seems as if the blood of Cain found its way through the flood.

The Fathers of...

As a fan of world mythology, the "three brothers" construct is used again and again and again (heck: Seth, Cain, Abel). In many of these legends, the three brothers represent distinct styles and differences. Lamech's boys seem to follow suit.

REALISM. For the realist, the boys represent different nations, and ignoring the global aspects of the flood, they show the originals of the other people in the world. Considering the time period, it seems to summarize the development of humanity. We developed instruments and music. We learned metallurgy. We learned how to farm. Anthropologically, this could be a 10,000 to 100,000 year summary of Homo Sapien development.

FANTASY. Or the Mark of Cain doomed these guys to sub-human groups. These are the light elves (music), Dark Elves (tents=darkness), and dwarves (metals). These are the monsters that prey upon regular humans. In Norse mythology, we have the Aesir and the Vanir separated into separate global regions, and the Vanir represent this stained dark race. Just a thought.

LITERAL. It doesn't matter because the flood swept them all away. Except for the Naamah* incident, everything that breathed air died in the flood, so these three nations have a dead end. God mentions them to Noah to help understand the wickedness of the people. In other words, they weren't normal folks like Egyptians, Hebrews, and Ethiopians—they were the offspring of the Mark.

Characteristic B: A Murderer

By itself, this chapter of Genesis doesn't paint a very vivid picture, but once you do a little digging, you realize there is a done of mythology about this story. Old, old legends. First, let's just look at what it says in Genesis.

"I have slain a man": Well, that's pretty clear. Lamech killed somebody. He didn't even hide the fact. He gathered his wives and told them so. Yet he suddenly adds another detail.

"and a young man": Hold on. Two?! Now it's getting serious. Notice how there is no mention or reference to war or battle. This seems to be murder. Our Lamech is a serial killer?

The psychology here is interesting. The cops didn't come and knock on his door. Lamech seems to purposefully reveal to his wives that he's done this. Why? The wives learn their husband is a killer. Is it to intimidate? Show off? Brag? These murders are referenced as if in the past, so he's committed them without consequence.

The old, old legends I mentioned earlier surround "The Song of the Sword." This is quite a rabbit hole. For some, it is the title of this ancient poem describing Lamech. For others, it is the backstory that Genesis references. In the backstories, the details vary a bit, but the central detail is that Lamech was out hunting one day when he came across some sort of wildman beast. He followed. He acted. He killed. Ooops, it turned out to be Cain. In the accidental killing of Cain, Lamech is overcome, and upon clapping his mighty hands together, he accidentally kills his son, Tubalcain. Something like that.

Characteristic C: Blasphemy

Regardless of the two slain figures, the reaction from Lamech is what's so worthy to note. Yes, he brags and flexes, but notice where his mind goes: mocking. He brings up that Cain was cursed by God. Well, the Mark meant that anyone who hurt Cain would be cursed "sevenfold."

Apparently, Lamech bore this curse since he killed Cain. Cain is the first man he killed. Then he killed his son, which in his mind was even worse. So he reasons that his wickedness and curse will be seventy-seven fold.

When Cain killed Abel, God showed up.

When Lamech killed Cain…

Oh, that's Lamech's point: THERE IS NO GOD. Nothing happened to him. He killed a man and there was no Divine Judgment. He got away with it. Whether in the same moment or much later, he killed a second person. Nothing happened to him. So later, he calls his wives together to tell them what happened. He touched the hot stove and wasn't burned.

So why include this in Genesis?

God's "short version" of history still includes Lamech while introducing the flood. As much as the "Sons of God" and the Giants likely changed the game, the story of Lamech is equally important. This guy was wicked, and by allowing his sin to go unpunished, it seemingly grew. The result? The world was filled with violence, and they also turned their hearts from God. Lamech is the poster child for the pre-flood world.

An Antichrist?

The biggest problem with planting my flag upon the hill of Lamech is the literal destructive quality of the described flood. Modern scientists scoff at the details of the flood because that much water would simply NOT allow anything to survive. The humidity alone would make it impossible to breathe. The tidal forces created by the moon would scour the earth with each daily pass. Plugging the details of Genesis into the computer creates absurd levels of destruction.

It'd take a miracle to survive it in an Ark.

It also makes it problematic to find the Kingdom of Lamech.

Or Lamech himself.

My interpretation of Mr. Eight is that he's a genetic Frankenstein of the Seven Kings that came before him. By picking Lamech as King #1, I'm painting myself into a corner. How do you find genetic code from someone from before the flood?

Creation Scientists have no problems explaining what happened to the dinosaurs prior and during the flood, yet burying Lamech in a tomb that managed to survive the flood requires quite a bit of imagination and a whole lot of magic and chance.

My greatest ally in choosing Lamech are the heaps of mythology in the world that not only describe a flood and a wicked world, but in many cases, describe an evil figure who gets buried by the flood. I'll serve up an easy one: Norse Mythology.

Ragnarök is a great parallel to an era of fallen angels and giants, where a global disaster comes and cleanses the world. It has a couple of human survivors saved inside of a tree, but it also mentions that not all the gods and giants perished prior to the flood. Some of them survived, only to be buried alive.

That's the type of story prehistoric tribes were telling around the campfire.

Buried god stories spread over the world.

The Days of Noah

Lastly, I feel that God loves symbolism and foreshadowing too much for Him not to pick someone from the world before the flood. Genesis and Revelation are the two bookends of our human story, so ignoring this era would be a bit disappointing. If King Agag was one of the 7, I'd be very disappointed.

But Lamech? Dude, he's pretty EPIC, and imagination allows his evil kingdom in the Land of Nod to be a major factor in the flood. However, I didn't settle on Lamech until I'd done my research into King Nimrod.

Nimrod led me to my *Truth About the Head* theory.

Buckle up. Let's meet Nimrod.

CHAPTER FIVE

HEAD GAMES

If the legends and lore surrounding Lamech were thin, well...Nimrod is FAT with legends and lore. The amount of material surrounding him was quite impressive, and in doing studies into the time period, things kept coming back to him again, and again, and again.

So who is Nimrod?

Like Lamech, he's another "prehistoric" king, which doesn't necessarily mean he's a caveman but that we didn't have modern historical records about him. Sure, we have Genesis, but the rest of the "facts" about him come from interpretations of mythology and archaeology. For someone writing a research paper, this is problematic. For me, it's perfect!

The first thing to know about Nimrod involves the time period. He's born AFTER the flood and is listed as the great-grandson of Noah. Being born AFTER the flood means we're dealing with the same world, the same geography, and the same civilizations we have when real historians show up. While the timeline isn't written in stone, it gives some specific years and details to show he was the great-grandson of Noah, so when you match up other genealogies, and factor in the B.C. dates from the historians, you get a rough birthdate of ABOUT 2,000 BC.

There are some Christian scholars who INSIST on these genealogies as being hyperbolic, which means they are exaggerated or symbolic of eras. Could be. This hyperbolic interpretation allows human history to stretch back thousands to millions of years if each name is an era. A literal interpretation of the timeline means the flood happened ABOUT 2,400 BC, so the world of Nimrod would be in that "rebuild" phase. For a few centuries, it was the Wild Wild West.

Here is how Genesis 10 describes Nimrod:

> **[Gen 10:1] Now these are the generations of the sons of Noah, Shem, Ham, and Japheth: and unto them were sons born after the flood. [6] And the sons of Ham; Cush, and Mizraim, and Phut, and Canaan. [7] And the sons of Cush; Seba, and Havilah, and Sabtah, and Raamah, and Sabtecha: and the sons of Raamah; Sheba, and Dedan. [8] And Cush begat Nimrod: he began to be <u>a mighty one</u> in the earth. [9] He was a mighty <u>hunter</u> before the LORD: wherefore it is said, Even as Nimrod the mighty hunter <u>before</u> the LORD. [10] And the beginning of his kingdom was <u>Babel</u>, and Erech, and Accad, and Calneh, in the land of Shinar. [11] Out of that land went forth Asshur, and builded <u>Nineveh</u>, and the city Rehoboth, and Calah, [12] And Resen between Nineveh and Calah: the same is a great city. [13] And Mizraim begat Ludim, and Anamim, and Lehabim, and Naphtuhim, [14] And Pathrusim, and Casluhim, (out of whom came Philistim,) and Caphtorim.**

Chronicles even mentions him briefly:

[10] And Cush begat Nimrod: he began to be <u>mighty</u> upon the earth.

Nimrod the Mighty

If you're skimming through all the names in Genesis 10, it's easy to shrug off the significance of Nimrod and his mighty description. Remember mythology? Well, I've seen several Bible "scholars" who jump all over the concept of Nimrod being a hunter. Guess who else was a hunter during this time period? Orion!!! One quick look at the legends and "scholars" make note at the bottom of the page that Nimrod was from the legendary era described in Greek Mythology. After all, when Homer wrote it down in 800 BC, he was describing stuff that happened centuries earlier. Orion was mighty. Orion was a hunter. Orion=Nimrod. Sure.

Having already done a study on King David and "Giants," I sat up when I came across the old Hebrew word גִּבֹּר־ (g̅ib ·bōr-). Ooh, cool word, huh? This word pops up again and again in association with GIANTS. Remember the (Angels + Women=Giants) stuff from Genesis 6? The children were described as gibbor. Now, I'm not going to ignore the fact that the word gibbor is used synonymous with warriors elsewhere. Yet it seems that this word became an epic metaphor. Instead of saying he was a literal evil donkey, he was metaphorically an evil donkey (B.A.). During the time of King David, when he was literally hunting giants, he assembled a team of giant killers. The name of his crack kill squad: the GIBBOR. So literally and figurative, the word Gibbor has connections to giants.

So Nimrod was a GIBBOR that hunted?

Or did Nimrod hunt GIBBOR?

Both theories work. It's the mythology era, after all.

Nimrod the Architect

Even though Chronicles shrugs it off, Genesis goes deeper into the fact that Nimrod was a builder. Now, even though I grew up in the country, I have nothing against cities. Yet cities are places of protection because you are afraid. You're afraid of the weather, other tribes, the wild animals, or those pesky giants that ate your cousins last week. Afraid. Being filled with fear makes you easy pickings for Satan.

Nineveh? Yep, a great city that existed for centuries but ultimately so filled with fear that Jonah chooses death rather than going there. Nimrod built many cities, but I assume fear was at the heart of it.

There are several names listed that are dead ends, but two names aren't: Babel and Mizraim. Mizraim might be a head scratcher, but it was the old term used for Egypt. You know Egypt: the place with amazing architecture. Yes, there are "scholars" out there who have speculated that the Egyptian builder IMHOTEP might also be NIMROD since the two eras overlap so closely. Imhotep=Nimrod? If so, then it explains how the pyramids suddenly popped up with an almost divine precision and perfection.

Yet Nimrod built something much more impressive than a pyramid. What's the city of Babel famous for? A tower. Okay, it doesn't actually SAY IT, but a few verses down, it does give the TOWER OF BABEL story. Lore connects the rest.

So if IMHOTEP=NIMROD=TOWER, we should take a peek at what some of the lore says about this time period. There was an ancient historian named Berossus who wrote about ancient times, and his lost works were referenced by other historians (Hey! No smoking inside the Library of Alexandria! How many times must I warn you kids?). His "accounts" are kinda goofy and fun.

Ready?

According to Berossus, the Tower of Babel was built by creatures known as the Annunaki, who are described as giants. That's right. Human bulldozers. His account also goes on to say that Pandora (the gal with the box) was a daughter-in-law of Noah. Huh? Also, he mentions that along with the tower, another ancient monument, Esagila, was built during this time period. It's name translates as "House of the Raised Head." We'll get back to that later.

Now, there are other accounts that connect Nimrod to the Tower of Babel, but this one involves GIBBOR. Does that mean Nimrod WAS a giant? Or does that mean that Nimrod wasn't just skilled at hunting elk and possum but also GIBBOR. If he was famous for hunting giants, what did he do with these giants? He enslaved them and forced them to build stuff like the Tower of Babel, cities, and the pyramids. How Norse is that? How Ancient Aliens is that?

The Tower of Nimrod

Okay, Genesis doesn't connect the dots for us. It mentions Nimrod. Words, words, words. Then it mentions the Tower of Babel. Now, just based on lifespans and generations, you can easily speculate that the founder of Babel would still be around during the construction of the Tower. If we set the flood date at 1656 (AC=After Creation), then Arphaxad was born in 1658 and lived until 2096 since he lived 438 years. Noah's great-grandson? Salah born in 1693, lived 433 years, thus dies in 2126. Great-grandson? Eber born 1723, lives 464, dies 2187. Nimrod is born during this time period, which means he could've ruled for hundreds of years. Want a wacky fact? Abraham (10 generations later) was born in 2008. Noah died in 2006! There is some MAJOR overlap going on.

There'd also be a population boom. Each generation "loses ground" on the lifespan battle until we finally arrive at "normal" humans following Abraham. Notice how the Genesis narrative goes from the Tower of Babel and right into the tale of Abraham. I believe it's because Abraham was alive and active during the Tower of Babel incident. He leaves Ur (Babel) because of Nimrod and the Tower. (That's another Bible study).

So when you picture the Tower Narrative, read it with both Nimrod and Abram in mind:

[Genesis 11:1] And the whole earth was of one language, and of one speech. [2] And it came to pass, as they journeyed from the east, that they found a plain in the <u>land of Shinar</u>; and they dwelt there. [3] And they said one to another, Go to, let us make brick, and burn them thoroughly. And they had brick for stone, and slime had they for mortar. [4] And they said, Go to, let us build us a city and a tower, whose top may reach unto heaven; and let us make us a name, <u>lest we be scattered</u> abroad upon the face of the whole earth. [5] And the LORD came down to see the city and the tower, which the children of men builded. [6] And the LORD said, Behold, the people is

one, and they have all one language; and this they begin to do: and now <u>nothing will be restrained from them</u>, which they have imagined to do. [7] Go to, let us go down, and there confound their language, that they may not understand one another's speech. [8] So the LORD scattered them abroad from thence upon the face of all the earth: and they left off to build the city. [9] Therefore is the name of it called Babel; because the LORD did there confound the language of all the earth: and from thence did the LORD scatter them abroad upon the face of all the earth.

Okay, so the nuts and bolts of this is that God wanted them to spread out over Earth 2.0; the people said no; built a tower; and then God showed up and said "you're going."

For me, there's a TON of unanswered questions in this section of text that has nothing to do with the mysteries of the language.

What's the rush?

Who united them?

Why a tower?

The Days of Peleg

The answer to question #1 is actually provided in Genesis (albeit not directly). When you look at the lifespans, you can see that something dramatic happens during generation 5. Peleg's lifespan is cut in half. While generation 6 and 7 follow suit, it drops again, and after Abraham, things get to a normal 120ish cap. My speculation is that the environment changed dramatically. Heck, to believe in the flood, I have to speculate A TON of dramatic climate change involving ice ages (for the flood waters), earthquakes, erosion, and…rising sea levels.

Both Genesis and Chronicles associate Peleg with "the earth was divided." Huh? There is a couple ways you could take this phrase. Are we talking Babel=language division? That certainly does the trick. But remember, God only messed with language because he had a reason for them to rush. So I think the dividing of the earth means geography. When I was a kid, I'd often marvel at the continental shelf and ponder a world with slightly lower water levels. (As an adult, I ponder rising ocean levels and imagine the inverse). Perhaps the Days of Peleg means that something really bad happened (huge volcano? Meteor? temperatures) that caused the ice caps to melt and glug, glug, glug…fill the world up to its recently stable status quo.

God gave Noah's family a few basic commands:

Be fruitful.

Spread out!

So when Nimrod's generation said NOPE, God had to get involved before the clock ran out. In this most conservative of timelines, humanity only had a few hundred years between the flood and the Peleg disaster to get to "land bridge" places like Australia, England, and America.

Who and why?

My answer wasn't found in legends and lore. Instead, it was found in "historical" documents. I "tease" history often since history is written by the conquerors in most cases, but 2,000 years ago, there was a Roman/Jewish historian named Josephus who wrote a HUGE book on the history of the world from a Jewish perspective. Granted, you never know how much is accurate, but it nevertheless, gives fantastic insight into what folks thought back in the time of Jesus. As it turns out, Josephus has a BIG explanation for the Tower of Babel.

"Now the plain, in which they first dwelt, was called Shinar. God also commanded them to send colonies abroad, for the thorough peopling of the earth; that they might not raise seditions among themselves, but might cultivate a great part of the earth, and enjoy its fruits after a plentiful manner. But they were so ill instructed, that they did not obey God. For which reason they fell into calamities, and were made sensible by experience of what sin they had been guilty of. For when they flourished with a numerous youth, God admonished them again to send out colonies. But they imagining the prosperity they enjoyed was not derived from the favor of God, but supposing that their own power was the proper cause of the plentiful condition they were in, did not obey him. Nay they added to this their disobedience to the divine will, the suspicion that they were therefore ordered to send out separate colonies, that, being divided asunder, they might the more easily be oppressed.

2. Now it was Nimrod who excited them to such an affront and contempt of God. He was the grand-son of Ham, the son of Noah: a bold man, and of great strength of hand. He persuaded them not to ascribe it to God, as if it was through his means that they were happy; but to believe that it was their own courage which procured that happiness. He also gradually changed the government into tyranny; seeing no other way of turning men from the fear of God, but to bring them into a constant dependence on his own power. He also said, "He would be revenged on God, if he should have a mind to drown the world again: for that he would build a Tower too high for the waters to be able to reach; and that he would avenge himself on God for destroying their forefathers.""

3. Now the multitude were very ready to follow the determination of Nimrod, and to esteem it a piece of <u>cowardice to submit</u> to God: and they built a Tower; neither sparing any pains, nor being in any degree negligent about the work. And, by reason of the multitude of hands employed in it, it grew very high, sooner than any one could expect. But the thickness of it was so great, and it was so strongly built, that thereby its great height seemed, upon the view, to be less than it really was. It was built of burnt brick, cemented together with mortar, made of bitumen; that it might not be liable to admit water. When God saw that they acted so madly, he did not resolve to destroy them utterly; since they were not grown wiser by the destruction of the former sinners: but he caused a tumult among them, by producing in them diverse languages; and causing, that through the multitude of those languages, they should not be able to understand one another. The place wherein they built the Tower is now called Babylon: because of the confusion of that language which they readily understood before: for the Hebrews mean by the word Babel, Confusion. <u>The Sibyll also makes mention</u> of this tower, and of the confusion of the language when she says thus: "When all men were of one language, some of them built an high tower, as if they would thereby ascend up to heaven. But the Gods sent storms of wind, and overthrew the tower, and gave everyone his peculiar language. And for this reason it was that the city was called Babylon." But as to the plain of Shinar, in the country of Babylonia, <u>Hestiæus</u> mentions it, when he says thus, "Such of the Priests as were saved took the sacred vessels of Jupiter Enyalius, and came to Shinar of Babylonia."

Wow, Josephus includes all sorts of stuff that Genesis didn't mention. Why? He's not making stuff up. Look how he ends: he cites sources. Just like I discovered, there's a ton of old legends and lore involving Nimrod, and Josephus just summarizes these tales. So what did we learn in the opening part?

God wanted folks to spread out on the earth.

Folks willfully disobeyed.

Nomads=faithful ☺

City builders=bad ☹

Why? They believed in God but distrusted him because of the flood.

So…Nimrod uses this to unify them. Apparently, Nimrod is a mighty warrior, and as the biggest, baddest guy in the room, he acts as a bully.

Then things get REALLY, REALLY dark. These folks readily believe God is real, but they blame him for what happened in the flood. They distrust him. They assume he'll do it again. So…behind Nimrod's leadership, they plan to KILL GOD!!!

Yes, the Tower is a type of flood insurance. They build it so if it floods again, they'll be able to climb up in it to escape the water. I guess this motivation explains WHY they built a tower. Nimrod doesn't just use slave labor; he gets volunteers who are afraid of drowning.

Yet they have another motivation for building the tower. God lives in Heaven, right? Heaven is up, right? God used to speak to Adam and Eve through a Window in Heaven, right? God opened a Window in Heaven to flood the world, right? So Nimrod does some calculating and decides that if they build this epic ladder, they'll be able to INVADE Heaven and "**avenge himself on God.**" This sounds like some bad Marvel Comics plot.

(If you're looking for a qualification to be the Antichrist, this move seems to be enough.)

Ultimately, Nimrod's "KILL GOD" plan is defeated by... God. By defeating them with language, our differences suddenly keep us from uniting against our creator. God distracts us and we turn on each other. We deserved a spanking for this, and he spanks us with language. Ironic punishment. God decided it wasn't time to have "An Emperor of the World" and saved that for the End Times, when language will no longer be an impediment thanks to Google Translate.

General Abram the Tank

Genesis doesn't give much clarity about Nimrod's role in the Tower incident nor does it give much clarity about this era's #1 Hero: Abram. Where was Abram born? Babel. Where did Nimrod rule? Babel. The Abram story begins without motivation as we see him packing up his family and moving several hundred miles away from Babel.

What's going on in Babel?

Nimrod stuff.

There's an entire book worth of stuff about Abram vs. Nimrod, but for the sake of brevity, I'll save that for another day. Just know that in his youth, Abram is neck deep in his opposition to Nimrod. It reads just like Moses vs. Pharaoh. In fact, there is even a popular Spanish folk song that tells the story of Nimrod and Abraham. It's lyrics are:

"When King Nimrod went out in the fields

Looked at the heavens and the stars

He saw a holy light in the Jewish quarter

A sign that Abraham, our father, was about to be born."

Strangely, when we are introduced to Abram in Genesis 12, he's being rewarded by God with the promise that God will "make thee a great nation." Aside from being born in Ur/Babel, what did he do to warrant this? See, it doesn't explain the early years of Abram at all, does it? While folks in Spain were singing the answer, I was scratching my head in South Dakota trying to understand the early motivations and deeds of Abram. What did this guy do?

That Spanish song is rooted in Hebrew legends and lore. You know…mythology. These are tales that are as old as the Trojan War and the Olympians, but it doesn't mean any of this stuff is accurate. Get my drift? These accounts are found in the Talmud and Pseudo-Philo. I include it because this odd puzzle piece seems to fit other legends.

A recap:

- Nimrod's grandfather tries to kill him at birth. Yeesh!
- Nimrod marries a woman named Semiramis (evil alert, evil alert!)
- A portent (sign/omen) predicts the birth of Abram.
- Abram's mother escapes and secretly gives birth (Bethlehem copyright?)
- Abram recognizes God from early age (despite growing up in Ur/Babel).
- Round 1: God sends Abram to warn Nimrod about idolatry.
- Round 2: Nimrod gathers wood for 4 years and then burns Abram.
- The fires do not harm Abram.

- Round 3: Nimrod fights Abram in open battle (General Abram?).
- Despite inferior numbers, God destroys Nimrod's forces with army of gnats.
- And…a gnat goes in Nimrod's brain and drives him crazy.
- As a peace treaty, Nimrod gives Abram his slave, Eliezer.
- Abram leaves Mesopotamia for "Promised Land."

Too good to be true? Perhaps. But it does "expand" a bunch of things that we find in Genesis that have no set up or explanation. Remember Abraham's "heir" problems. The parts about Ishmael and Isaac are often discussed, but if you look closely, he almost promotes Eliezer (not a relative) as his heir. Who? The folklore explains where this guy came from—Nimrod.

Shortly after Abram settles in Canaan, Lot is taken prisoner during the War of the Nine Kings. Who are these guys? Where did they come from? I'm betting that these guys are the former allies of Abram when he went to war with Nimrod. After the successful war with Nimrod, they clean up the giants before turning on each other in the vacuum left by Nimrod. In this chaos, Lot is taken prisoner. When Rambo…er…Abraham learns his nephew has been kidnapped, he puts on his war paint, unburies the hatchet, and whoops some. Abraham has MAD MILITARY skillz. How'd he acquire those? See the above story.

So somewhere in all of this "early life" plot of Abram, the Tower of Babel happens. It makes sense to happen during this time period. This leaves Nimrod totally defeated and without a Tower or Army. Just like God drew Moses from the water to deal with Pharaoh, it seems Abram is the counterweight to evil Nimrod.

Mapping Nimrod's Mythology

Time to roll up my sleeves. One of the games/activities that I always played in my mythology class was the "Farmer in Western Kansas" activity where you read a two-paragraph story about a farmer, a tornado, and a bad dad joke. Like the phone game, each kid would pass the story to the next "blind" listener and so forth. I liked it because it replicated how a FACT could be dramatically changed by omission and addition. By the time we got to the final "contemporary" tale-teller, the story was a hot mess. Yet at its core…bits of truth.

I feel there are bits of truth about Nimrod found in all of these legends. The names and details get changed, but they all seem to be telling the same story. I'll go through them in no particular order.

Pirke De-Rabbi Eliezer: In this telling, there is a fascinating connection to the pre flood world. In it, Nimrod inherits <u>the garments of Adam and Eve</u>. Remember the fruit? Well, shortly after Adam and Eve ate it, God called them together and…naked. So He does something wise and horrible—he clothes them. How? He kills one of his creations to clothe them. Were these magical, immortal animals? Heck, they might've been the original unicorns! (Not a Rhino). Regardless, these garments were passed down, brought on the Ark, and then found their way into the hands of…a HUNTER. Ah, that's dark symbolism. Later in this narrative, Nimrod <u>defeats the armies of Japheth</u> to create universal rule, which makes him the original

Emperor of the Earth. The ending of the narrative is a tad odd. In it, Esau ambushes him, robs him, and then beheads him. This reminds me a lot of the Cain/Lamech narrative. The BE-HEADING is also a dark rabbit hole theory I'll get to in a bit.

Kitab al-Magall is an Arabic narrative. In this tale, Nimrod has magic. The non-Biblical 4th son of Noah, Bouniter, teaches young Nimrod the powers of divination. What's that? Looking into the future...might've motivated Nimrod the same way it motivated Nebuchadnezzar. Seeing the bookend prophecy involving fire or the Antichrist might've made him motivated to change the future and...voila! The Tower of Babel plan. This narrative builds on the idea that Nimrod was an engineer and architect that created cities. The most unique aspect was that as the "first king" he also chose to wear a crown. Pause. Why do we wear crowns? (scratching skull). Halo! Wow, we're trying to restore our former glow OR we're trying to appear like the angels. Nimrod wears a halo to spite his mortality and to celebrate his lost divinity. Not only does Nimrod create the "crown" concept but then he creates a flag: a piece of black cloth with his golden crown upon it.

(STRAY THEORY: Gold is precious. Science believes gold is alien to earth and was created by a supernova that scattered traces of it throughout the universe. Translation: It's special. Reading the Ethiopian tales of creation, it seems GOLD was a vital part of Eden and the Holy Mountain of God. Want something Biblical? Read Ezekiel 28:13-14. My point is...the Holy Mountain of God was destroyed by the flood and...the GOLD was scattered. How Nimrod-y would it be to gather up that gold? Each fleck is a reminder of what we lost.)

Speaking of…

Conflict of Adam and Eve with Satan is that Ethiopian version of Genesis that I've referenced prior. Again, it has all sorts of stray theories and concepts, and in it, it mentions Santal who is a "crown maker" and is taught by Noah's fourth son, this time named Barvin. What's up with that 4th son?

The Cave of Treasures is an Arabic text that's old yet recently discovered, making it…apocryphal and pseudepigraphical. Yet it adds to the legend by mentioning the 4th Son of Noah. In this story, he is named Yontan. So…something major certainly happened during this 4th generation, which is when Nimrod ruled. While we don't get much about Nimrod, we also get another crown story. In this narrative, Sisan is credited as being the original weaver of a crown.

The Book of Recognitions comes close to being a Nimrod story. In this Greek text, it describes King Ninus who rules Assyria. Where is Assyria? Yup, the Tigris and Euphrates place just like ancient Babel. Oh, and it says that Ninus was the guy who founded Ninevah. So…Ninus=Nimrod. Got it. The most interesting tidbit brought up by this text is that King N is the origin story of Zoroaster. Who? Oh, baby. Zoroaster (also known as Zarathustra) is the founder of an ancient religion with origins thousands of years BC (that places us in Nimrod's era). Zoroastrianism is not only a religion that survives to today but its theories go all over the place. I've come across Zoroaster lore when reading Alchemy origin stories and also when reading Christian, Jewish, and Islamic theories about those "founding fathers" of Genesis 10. If Nimrod did indeed become an Emperor who was defeated by God/Abram, then his followers likely would not have simply "let it go." Stuff for thought, here.

Abu al-Fida adds that in the language reset, Eber (Hebews) got to keep the original language since they didn't give aid to the building of the tower. In that account, it establishes that Nimrod rules for 500 years and introduced the fundamentals of astrology. This narrative also builds on the legend of Abram, which has Nimrod trying to "Herod" the child.

A ***Hungarian Legend*** has some fascinating information. In this account, they use the name Menrot when describing him, but build on the idea that Nimrod was in fact a literal giant. Their story is about how Kam became the father of the Hungarians and involves a legend of the White Stag. Anyway, it adds that the Tower was built 201 years after the flood. Kam and his wife En move to a place called Evalit where they give birth to twins, Hunor and Magyar. These boys go on to become the founding fathers of the Huns and Hungarians. During the hunt for the White Stag, Esau is brought up again as the guy who kills and beheads Nimrod. The repetition of Esau is curious, and so too is the "beheaded" legend, which I'll get to later.

Tidbits

There are a few more random tales that I found interesting that pile on a few more details and theories. Ninus=Zoroaster=Sargon=Marduk=Ninurta=Baal=Osiris=Belus =etc. It's a fat legend.

Safer ha Yashar adds a detail that Nimrod's son is named Mardon and is "made wicked." We'll circle back to the child of Nimrod detail.

The <u>History of the Prophets and Kings</u> text echoes the idea that Nimrod was the builder of the tower of Babel and that "Allah destroyed it." Now, this fires up an interesting thought: If the tower was big enough to reach the window of heaven, what happened after the language snafu? Nothing is mentioned in Genesis. Earthquake? Lightning storm?

The Armenians mention that Hayk defeated Nimrod but also associate the name Bel (which is another rabbit hole).

The Qur'an adds the detail that Nimrod released two death sentence prisoners.

Finally, <u>Ephrem the Syrian</u> flips the script and says Nimrod was righteous and didn't want the Tower. (Always another POV, huh?)

So you can see the tip of this iceberg. At one point, Nimrod was a known villain. He's seeped into our culture through Bugs Bunny who called Elmer Fudd (a hunter) a Nimrod. Freemason lore credits Nimrod as one of the fraternity's founders. Dante mentions Nimrod in this section on giants. The rest faded into oblivion. Yet the most alarming of all these tales is the implication of his wife. Let's meet the Mrs.

The "Original" Queen of Heaven

The prophet Jeremiah knows the story. He understands the horrible line that the Hebrews crossed when they worshiped the gods of their enemies. In fact, he brings up she-who-shall-not be-named during one of his famous chides:

> **[Jeremiah 44:15] Then all the men which knew that their wives had burned incense unto other gods, and all the women that stood by, a great multitude, even all the people that dwelt in**

the land of Egypt, in Pathros, answered Jeremiah, saying, [16] As for the word that thou hast spoken unto us in the name of the LORD, we will not hearken unto thee. [17] But we will certainly do whatsoever thing goeth forth out of our own mouth, to burn incense unto <u>the queen of heaven</u>, and to pour out drink offerings unto her, as we have done, we, and our fathers, our kings, and our princes, in the cities of Judah, and in the streets of Jerusalem: for then had we plenty of victuals, and were well, and saw no evil. [18] But since we left off to burn incense to the <u>queen of heaven</u>, and to pour out drink offerings unto her, we have wanted all things, and have been consumed by the sword and by the famine. [19] And when we burned incense to the <u>queen of heaven</u>, and poured out drink offerings unto her, did we make her cakes to worship her, and pour out drink offerings unto her, without our men?

Jeremiah believes that the bad stuff happening is all because folks worshiped the Queen of Heaven. So who is she?

From what I've found, the source for this legend goes back to the Queen of Babel, the wife of King Nimrod, a woman named Semiramis. Because...

If Nimrod=Ninus=Zoroaster=Osiris=Imhotep=Baal then...

Semiramis=Isis=Ishtar=Astarte=Anath=Kali!

Now, with an equation like the one above, you must understand that there are no hard facts with mythology. I only began my study of this time period in recent years, and sure enough, there were plenty of scholars before me trying to connect the equation Nimrod+Semiramis=trouble. There is actually much more archaeological backstory for her than there is for Nimrod.

The story behind Semiramis is that she had a divine origin. Apparently, she had some sort of fish-goddess mother. Remember this when we get to a later chapter. Fishmom. Well,

Fishmom abandons her child in a field, and a mythological miracle happens: the Artist Formerly Known as Prince saves her. Kinda. Well, not really, but at the sound of crying, doves show up, and you know, bring her food. Prince? (I try). In another mythology trope, a lonely farmer stumbles across poor Semiramis and finds the child.

Later, she upgrades and marries a warrior. This warrior eventually becomes the right hand man of King Nimrod. Problem! Nimrod lusts after her, and in classic David-Bathsheba-Uriah storytelling, Nimrod pressures the guy until he commits suicide. Then Nimrod marries her.

Now, just like the Tower of Babel story indicates, their empire expands. Her name and likeness is carved into ancient buildings all over the region. Her M.O. is the seduce and (if denied) conquer any rival kings (see Ara the Handsome). So both her sexuality and warrior status spreads through the region. Ironically, despite her rampant sexuality, she's often portrayed as a virgin warrior. Virgin warrior? Yep, many scholars believe she is the inspiration behind deities like Athena, Anath, and Kali. Again, if folks in this era live for a few hundred years, it makes sense why her reign of conquests lasted 42 years and she conquered a triangle of territory ranging from Libya to Ethiopia to India.

Her influence is also seen during her reign. She instituted the concept of castration for her male priests, child sacrifices, and chastity belts. Her religion included the concept of confession since she was a medium (go between) to the gods. To maintain power, she created a secret society within normal society. Yep, the original Deep State.

If it wasn't dark enough, things take a dramatically dark twist. In the middle of her reign, Nimrod dies in private. The general public doesn't know their king is dead. Did I forget to tell you that several years earlier, she and Nimrod had a son, which she secretly kept hidden from the public? Why would she do that? (muh, ha, ha). Her grand scheme was to show the power of resurrection. Once she got things ready, she "revealed" to her people that King Nimrod was indeed dead. She likely proved it to them by burning him on a pyre, and then…presto! She brings him back to life again (in the form of their son). Nimrod 2.0!!!

And then she commits incest with her son/prince. We'll hear this again in a later chapter with another "Queen of Heaven" story. Now this is where other mythologies come into play. In Egyptian Mythology, Isis loses her husband Osiris, collects his body parts, and presto! Osiris 2.0. In Canaanite mythology, Anath loses her brother, she collects his body parts, he transforms into a bull (Exodus golden calf), rapes her, and her child becomes…Baal 2.0. The ancient art is all over the place when you see the Queen suckling her prince. The Isis and Horus/Osiris art later became synonymous with the Madonna and Child (eww, I know. Painters!!!).

Prior to (Shem) killing Nimrod, she had secretly given birth to his child. In resurrecting "Nimrod," she took child as husband

So while all this is going on, you have the Tower of Babel, the Days of Peleg, and Abram running around. Pretty intense era, huh?

The House of the Raised Head

As interesting as I find Nimrod and Semiramis, there are a few aspects that especially resonate with me. I discovered these mysterious aspects when I was reading about Alexander the Great. In his chapter, he conquered the region and when he gets to Babylon, he suddenly fixates on a few items. One of his projects was the restoration of Esagila.

Esagila?

Well, it turns out that it doesn't really matter because as soon as Alexander returns from his trip to India, he gets poisoned and his right-hand man not only executes his family but also undoes all the work made on Esagila.

Oh, now I really need to know more about Esagila. You?

The wildest thing about Ancient Babylon is that its history can be easily located. To find Esagila, you start at ancient Babylon, where you can still find the Ishtar Gate and the general area for the Hanging Gardens of Babylon…err…strike that, according to Diodorus, they were originally called the Hanging Gardens of Semiramis. Recognize her? Anyway, go south, past the Etemenanki, which is rumored to be the inspiration for the Tower of Babel story. Yep. Just a bit past that, you'll find the dust and rubble belonging to Esagila.

The term Esagila has a few translation variations. Some believe it translates as "temple whose top is lofty" which certainly has Tower of Babel tones. The more curious translation is "house of the raised head." The earliest builders believed the location belonged to the gods, and thus, they deserved to have a new temple built there, and…to build it tall enough to raise that head up where it belongs.

Rather than just shrugging and chalking it all up to Tower of Babel lore, I kept going down the rabbit hole. In my literary journey for my book series, I went down the alchemy rabbit hole, which included the Templars and Baphomet, but in generation after generation, these folks kept using a severed head metaphor. They even appropriated John the Baptist to "hide" their symbols out in public. It's a deep rabbit hole. Remember Nimrod lore fixating on him getting beheaded? Worshiping the severed head had an origin, and it seems to go back to Babylon.

God used the flood to "cleanse" a corrupt world, right?

Yet within four generations, it all fell apart and He had to intervene with the Tower of Babel. So what went so wrong so quickly?

Esagila!

Just hearing the term "House of the Raised Head" made me think of a giant (large) head that once belonged to an even larger statue. Any city or statue made before the flood would've been destroyed, right? In the mirky lore surrounding Esagila, there are stories about "discovering" the head and "restoring" an ancient temple. My big problem is I'm seeing this time period through the lens of a Creationist whose most literal interpretation of Biblical chronology means that Nimrod stuff happened just a few hundred years after a global flood. Anything that anybody discovers from this era came from the preflood world.

Oh...that would do it.

Imagine discovering the Santa beard in your parents' dresser drawer. Dad? Well, the same reality-shattering discovery would happen if you found evidence of an older world destroyed by the flood. Who were these people? What happened to them? Why would God kill them all?

Now, reread Nimrod's motivation.

I believe he discovered some relic that motivated him to build the Tower to avenge himself on God. That, folks, is a prime Antichrist candidate. Imagine this: Lamech's face is on the statue. So Nimrod dives into the "Sons of Perdition" legends and lore and decides to build a shrine to King/Head #1. The shrine is Esagila, the House of the Raised Head. Does my theory hold any water?

Josephus gave me a cool nugget of support. This is what he wrote:

"But as to the plain of Shinar, in the country of Babylonia, Hestiæus mentions it, when he says thus, 'Such of the Priests as were saved took the sacred vessels of Jupiter Enyalius, and came to Shinar of Babylonia.'"

Priests? This is long before God pegged Aaron for the Levitical priesthood. What if these guys were "bad" priests? These were Tower of Babel priests, after all. These guys had "sacred vessels." What are these? Again, the Creationist lens has Noah getting off the Ark at Ararat just a few generations earlier. Nimrod is his great-grandson. This is a narrow window of time, and within it, we have priests with "vessels" traveling to Shinar, where Esagila will be built.

A big problem is that 2400 BC predates Greek and Roman mythology. There hasn't even been time for the Greek language to be created. Yet Hestiæus writes that a group of priests traveled with vessels dedicated to Jupiter Enyalius. What's up with that? Now, Jupiter is an easy one. That's the Roman (who didn't exist yet) name for Zeus, the God of Up. Whoa. Up is lofty. While the name Lamech certainly wasn't used, Jupiter is a murderous (Lamech) god who killed his own father (Cain) to rule the world. The other word? Enyalius is VERY obscure. Current Greek/Roman mythology has him listed as a minor god connected to Ares, yet the word means "warlike" or "the spirit of war." So the priests had some vessel that led them to where they found a statue of a warlike, father-murdering king.

"We'll build the Tower of Babel here!

Gather up some men!

We're retaking heaven and killing God."

That, folks, is my candidate #2.

Nimrod is King #2.

CHAPTER SIX

THE SON OF PERDITION HAS NO SOUL

According to legend, the mightiest of the Canaanite gods was Baal the storm god. While the Greeks had Zeus and his lightning bolts and the Norse had Thor and his thunderous hammer, the folks who moved into the Promised Land worshiped Baal. It's hard to understand the allure of Baal today, but apparently, Baal was an addiction worthy of rotting teeth and an RV full of stolen chemistry lab equipment. Addictive stuff. Instead of returning after Joseph's famine, the Hebrews chose to stay in Egypt rather than returning to face these fellows, and when they did...whew, doggie. What happened to the Promised Land? Remember those giants from Lamech's era? Oh yes, they were back.

Yet the most telling terror tale of the tyrannical nature of Baal worship is found in the origin of Baal's nick-name...Beelzebub. Many folks think this is a nickname for Satan, but Jesus clarifies that they are two separate entities during his "House Divided" conversation with some exorcists. Baal got the name Beelzebub because of the Hebrews, who after 40 years of time out (not wandering) in the desert, finished the trip. All the folks who freaked out with the Golden Calf (Baal's symbol) had aged-out and a young generation raised on faith and manna marched on the Promised Land.

On the borders of the Promised Land, the Hebrew spies saw a strange anomaly. Markers dotted the horizon like a border. When they got closer, they realized the markers were not stacked stones…but bodies! To show their psychopathic toughness, the Baal worshippers hacked up their own children and placed them in piles. These rotting piles of bodies were gruesome, but what made it worse were the swarms of flies that feasted on the flesh of these children. How horrible! Baal=Beel=Lord. Flies=Zebub=Zebul. This "Lord of the Flies" became synonymous with Beelzebub and Baal.

And Baal's sister Anath was the evil one in the family.

Honoring Anath

So I wanted to start this chapter with a reminder about Anath. In Canaanite mythology, she is depicted as this virgin warrior goddess. In one classic scene, following an assassination of her brother, she hosts all of her enemies, secretly poisons them, locks the doors, and beheads them all and creates garlands of their hands to decorate the palace. Yikes! In an even more diabolical scene, she gathers up her brother's dismembered body, tosses them into a magical swamp, and voila! Her brother is reborn as a bull that subsequently rapes her. Vile stuff. Don't forget, many scholars believe the similarity between Anath, Kali,

Athena, etc., etc. is because they all originate with the older tale of Queen Semiramis.

Having seen Yule Brenner portray Ramses the Great, and much later Ralph Fiennes, the concocted brotherly relationship between he and Moses is almost charming.

A charming lie.

The Biblical Ramses is much different than the modernized portrayal. Oh, and for the record, I wrote **Examining Moses** to explain why I do in fact believe that Ramses the Great is the antagonist to Moses in Exodus. (So I'll be using the name Ramses the Great for THAT unnamed Pharaoh).

The most obscure clue about his evil connection?

He named his firstborn daughter after Anath.

What does that tell you?

For me, this little detail was discovered when I was trying to understand why Exodus 12:37 says "And the children of Israel journeyed from Rameses to Succoth" if the Pharaoh was somebody other than Ramses. After all, that'd be like Columbus showing up to America and a river already was named Columbia. Or having the capital being named Washington DC two hundred years before Washington was born. How can there be a city named Rameses if the dude hadn't been born yet? A lawyer can argue anything away, but I went with it. In sticking my nose into the history of the city, I discovered that Ramses the Great dedicated the city to his daughter Bith-Anath, which is a cute way of saying Daughter of Anath. While none of the ruins or relics mention anybody named Moses (why would they?), Ramses the Great has his daughter's name carved all over his new city in Goshen. Do you remember the 10th Plague? Notice how it doesn't say "firstborn son" like it shows in the movie. Instead it just says "firstborn" of any type of animal from human to dog. So the dedication likely happened after the 10th plague. See?

A Family Tradition

But something else that really bothered me is WHY WOULD A PHARAOH WORSHIP A FOREIGN GOD? While I'm not a PHD in Egyptian mythology, I've studied it for decades now. Even without Egyptian historical records (commissioned by Ramses the Great) mentioning Moses or the Hebrews, they do mention the Hyksos invasion that explains why Joseph's Pharaoh was a different dynasty than the Pharaoh of Moses. Classic Egyptian Mythology has gods like Ra, Osiris, Isis, Horus...those folks. Through the centuries, the gods shifted to Amen-Ra, Aten, Atum, and Bast (god of cats). Yet while the hero gods changed frequently, the evil gods and gods of death remained...Set, Anubis, Apophis, Nephthys, etc.

During the dark era of Hyksos control, those rulers worshiped Apophis, the serpent of destruction. Dark dudes. When the Theban Princes (old school Egyptians) rose up in rebellion and cast them out, it began a "Make Egypt Great Again" era. These MEGA-Pharaohs tried to purge Egypt of all foreigners (including the Hebrews). Yet after several rulers, a new crop came along.

Ramses the Great's dad?

Pharaoh Set(i)...named after the God of Evil.

That, folks, sets a different tone.

Rumor has it that the defeated Hyksos left Egypt and settled in...Canaan. Not only did they bring their former god Apophis with them, but now intermingled with the Canaanites, they adopted new names for an old story. Nimrod and Semiramis first became Osiris and Isis and now became Baal and Anath.

Ramses the Great's father was named after the God of Evil, and his daughter was named after Anath. See a pattern? And the most likely trait that makes him a candidate to be the antichrist?

He was a ginger!

I tease. While a forensic examination revealed this unique trait, it goes to show that the 19th Dynasty figures and some of the older 18th Dynasty figures were not traditionally Egyptian. Whether "lower" or "upper" Egyptians, Ramses and family attained power through marriage and murder and usurped control of the country. Who were they? Where did they come from? Not clear. While the Theban princes helped overthrow the Hyksos, Ramses and Company seem to overthrow those guys, so they don't seem to belong to the north or south. Were they "sea people" immigrants like the enigmatic Philistines? Were they holdovers from the Hyksos people? Were they hired servants connected to the neighboring Canaanites?

Weirdest theory: Ramses the Great and Moses are somewhere in the 15th to 13th Century BC range, and on the other side of the Mediterranean, the deeds of the Trojan War were likely happening during the same era. The House of Tantalus, noted for its red hair because of a curse due to cannibalism and kinslaying, eventually manifested itself as Agamemnon and Menelaus. In the texts of the Odyssey, Menelaus gets caught in a storm and is swept away to Egypt, where he is marooned for several years. Menelaus has red hair. So...there are some literary possibilities of some cursed, royal DNA arriving in Egypt about this time. Historically, Ramses the Great lived a long life and was the greatest pharaoh evaah. How do we know this? He had it written down.

In dreaming about 4 FUTURE heads (not the 3 in the past), Daniel gives some characterization about the antichrists to come.

[Daniel 7:25] And he shall speak great words against the most High, and shall wear out the saints of the most High, and think to change times and laws:

Changing times and laws. That's akin to rewriting history. So all the monuments and building projects that happen during this era have stories and histories written upon them. Well, what if Ramses the Great is a big, fat liar?

Moses and the Hebrews did not exist because there is no "proof" or "evidence" that they existed on the monuments created by Ramses the Great. See the problem? Historians have no issues ignoring Moses, yet they do admit to something interesting: Ramses the Great went out of his way to deface the Amarna Period from Dynasty 18. Who are they? Pharaoh Akhenaten and Queen Nefertiti. These guys promoted a "light" god over evil gods like Set and Anath. Oh, and they pushed monotheism also. Oh, Oh, and if Ramses the Great = Mr. Hard Heart Pharaoh, then 80 years earlier, these folks likely were the two who drew the infant Moses out of the Nile. Seriously, read my *Examining Moses* study for the whole theory. So if my theory is true, it would give Ramses the Great proper motivation to desecrate the graves and monuments of these figures. If you're going to erase the Hebrews, might as well erase the folks who took them into court.

Now that you see why Ramses the Great is on my radar for being Antichrist #3, let's take a look at some defining moments from the Bible that support this.

And in this Corner

When doing a study on End Times, Timothy doesn't pop up as an obvious source. Well, take a look at what Paul says to him in 2nd Timothy Chapter 3:

> **[2nd Tim 3:1] This know also, that <u>in the last days</u> perilous times shall come. [2] For men shall be lovers of their own selves, covetous, boasters, proud, blasphemers, disobedient to parents, unthankful, unholy, [3] Without natural affection, trucebreakers, false accusers, incontinent, fierce, despisers of those that are good, [4] Traitors, heady, high-minded, lovers of pleasures more than lovers of God; [5] Having a form of godliness, but denying the power thereof: from such turn away. [6] For of this sort are they which creep into houses, and lead captive silly women laden with sins, led away with divers lusts, [7] Ever learning, and never able to come to the knowledge of the truth. [8] <u>Now as Jannes and Jambres withstood Moses,</u> so do these also resist the truth: men of corrupt minds, reprobate concerning the faith. [9] But they shall proceed no further: for their folly shall be manifest unto all men, as theirs also was.**

I included the whole paragraph just so you can see another reason why I went with Ramses the Great. Paul starts it in a similar fashion to how Peter established flood=End Times. In this passage, he begins by describing the awfulness of the End Times, and then he finishes his point by saying all of this is JUST LIKE JANNES AND JAMBRES. Don't know those names, well, at least he gave us a connection by also stating the name of Moses also.

(rolling up my sleeves)

So who were Jannes and Jambres? Oh, baby. What a rabbit hole!

I'll cut to the chase: these guys were the sorcerers who turned their staffs into snakes. Before I go down the rabbit hole, let's look at that scene.

> **[Exodus 4:1] And Moses answered and said, But, behold, they will not believe me, nor hearken unto my voice: for they will say, The LORD hath not appeared unto thee. [2] And the LORD said unto him, What is that in thine hand? And he said, A rod. [3] And he said, Cast it on the ground. And he cast it on the ground, and it became a serpent; and Moses fled from before it. [4] And the LORD said unto Moses, Put forth thine hand, and take it by the tail. And he put forth his hand, and caught it, and it became a rod in his hand:**

This was done not long before Moses returned to Egypt, and in part, was done to show that it was God who was responsible for this "magic act" that we see here. Moses knows he can do it and also knows where the power comes from: God.

Here is how it goes down in:

> **[Exodus 7:8] And the LORD spake unto Moses and unto Aaron, saying, [9] When Pharaoh shall speak unto you, saying, Shew a miracle for you: then thou shalt say unto Aaron, Take thy rod, and cast it before Pharaoh, and it shall become a serpent. [10] And Moses and Aaron went in unto Pharaoh, and they did so as the LORD had commanded: and Aaron cast down his rod**

**before Pharaoh, and before his servants, and it became a
serpent. [11] Then Pharaoh also called the wise men and the
sorcerers: now the magicians of Egypt, they also did in like
manner with their enchantments. [12] For they cast down
every man his rod, and they became serpents: but Aaron's rod
swallowed up their rods. [13] And he hardened Pharaoh's
heart, that he hearkened not unto them; as the LORD had said.**

Say what? Unlike the cartoon I watched, these guys literally
turned their staffs into snakes. The illusion wasn't broken, or the
trick revealed. Aaron's snake ate their snakes. This wasn't a parable
about deceit or fraud. Real snakes. Obviously, Moses knew
about these guys ahead of time, which is why God proved it to
him before sending him back to Egypt. God had to show him
that he was THE GUY.

But what does this say about Jannes and Jambres?

Moses/Aaron does their trick first, which could be shocking.
It's one thing to hold a pencil in the middle and start to wiggle it.
This trick, however, transformed matter. Let it be real. Aaron,
after all, didn't have a hidden compartment that allowed a snake
to emerge and then hide the tube up his sleeve. Also, how would
Jannes and Jambres know they were going to do this specific
trick?

Ta-dah!

Yet a few seconds later. Presto! They pull of the same trick.
How are they doing this? By whose power do they perform this
miracle? Let's explore this thought.

Not only did Paul and Timothy know this story in the 1st
century AD, but most Hebrews knew it in their culture. Here's
other places they are mentioned:

The Apocryphon of Jannes and Jambres
The Testament of Solomon
Pliny the Elder's *Natural History*
The Gospel of Nicodemus
Eusebius' *Praeparatio Evangelica*
Babylonian Talmud
Targum Pseudo-Jonathan
Damascus Document
Questions of St. Bartholomew
Penitence of the Cyprian
Lausiac History

None of those sources are anything close to "Biblical" but it's interesting to know what these guys were well known and that is why Paul referenced them. Here's what you can glean about these guys

- From a sect of magicians
- Opponents of Moses
- They tried to undo the 10 plagues
- Called the Sons of Balaam
- Used powerful talismans
- Fought angels as they tried to enter Heaven
- Got to Level 5 of Heaven before being cast out by the Metatron
- In league with Belial

Priests of Perdition

The Belial connection is fascinating to me. In an earlier chapter, I attempted to explain that evil is more than just Satan. In fact, if you look at the end of Revelation, you discover that the

Antichrist, his prophet, and Satan are cast in the Lake of Fire yet two more enemies still exist: Death and Hades. To be brief, I feel Hades is akin to Beelzebub, the gatekeeper of the Underworld. Their big boss? Death. Now, there are a ton of mythological terms and names to be used but if you were to lump them all together with Biblical terms, here we go:

Perdition=Belial=Darkness=Death

Read the opening of John with the idea that the biggest, baddest enemy is NOT Satan but the big boss that opposes light.

> **[John 1:1] In the beginning was the Word, and the Word was with God, and the Word was God. [2] The same was in the beginning with God. [3] All things were made by him; and without him was not anything made that was made. [4] In him was life; and the life was the light of men. [5] And the light shineth in <u>darkness</u>; and the <u>darkness comprehended</u> it not.**

The opposite of life=

The opposite of light=

The opposite of the Word=

Notice how Death is personified. Death is more than just a concept. It is the opposition to all the good things listed above and below. So in Genesis 1:1, when God hovers over the face of the dark waters, He brings life and light to a dark universe. Yet the Universe opposes this idea. Darkness is the best metaphor. Here is another passage that openly compares these concepts again:

> **[2 Corinthians 6:14] Be ye not unequally yoked together with unbelievers: for what fellowship hath righteousness with unrighteousness? and what communion hath light with darkness? [15] And what concord hath Christ with Belial? or what part hath he that believeth with an infidel?**

The opposite of believer=

The opposite of righteousness=

The opposite of light=

The opposite of Christ=Belial

Yup. There it is. The fact that Jannes and Jambres were Priests of Belial means something MAJOR. This isn't a matter of evangelizing the Anishinaabe People, who already believe in a Great Spirit, a god-made-flesh Mediator, or even a helpful personal spirit guide. That's easy! Ramses worshiped some dark deities—from Anath to Belial.

So being a "Son of Perdition" might not just be a genetic family tree connection. It is also a spiritual choice. Lamech mocked God and chose the Darkness. Nimrod turned away from Noah's God and instead unearthed a "head" that led him into Darkness. Centuries later, Ramses the Great turns away from both the Hebrew God and the Egyptian gods and instead worships Darkness with new names.

Born Bad

There were a whole lot of reasons for God to send Christ to earth. One of the major reasons was to let a human institution created with 12 disciples evangelize the world. Humans would lead other humans back to the light. Our loving God is hoping to get as many as possible redeemed. Why? He loves us. He wants us back.

Yet when you look at the earlier passage, it mentioned how God **hardened Pharaoh's heart.** Instead of trying to redeem Ramses, God does the opposite. What's up with that? Remember Nebuchadnezzar? That guy got tormented and then flip-flopped. Ramses has neither flip nor flop.

The concept of PREDESTINATION, or God plotting our lives, really scrambles a person's brain. There are Bible verses to support it. There are Bible verses to oppose it. Of course I can imagine an EPIC God who has no problem plotting several billion plots at once. I can also imagine the importance of free will and choice. This is an unwinnable debate. Here's something to consider: What if God is predestining the BAD guys? The plot needs them. Humanity needs them to reach its final destination. Those seven ANTICHRISTS all serve a purpose. So before we return to discuss the hardening of hearts, let's look at how Jesus talked about 11 of his 12 disciples:

> **[John 17:9] I pray for them: I pray not for the world, but for them which thou hast given me; for they are thine. [10] And all mine are thine, and thine are mine; and I am glorified in them. [11] And now I am no more in the world, but these are in the world, and I come to thee. Holy Father, keep through thine own name those whom thou hast given me, that they may be one, as we are. [12] While I was with them in the world, I kept them in thy name: those that thou gavest me I have kept, and none of them is lost, but <u>the son of perdition</u>; that the scripture might be fulfilled.**

So this is the last supper, right after Judas left. Jesus knows it's his final night, and he prays for the 11 disciples who remain. He discusses a situation that sounds like there might've been a bit of doubt. God gave them. Jesus kept them. Not 1 of the 11 was lost. Was there any doubt, Jesus? Regardless, Jesus seems thankful to have reached this point.

But Judas?

Dang…

Jesus just called him a "son of perdition." (We'll come back to this in a later chapter). Yet instead of saying that he only lost 1 of 12, Jesus says that Judas doesn't count because he was never lost. He was always a "son of perdition" because scripture said he was. That's a bit of Predestination. Can't lose something you never had.

Ramses? He was never going to be persuaded to let the Hebrews go. Why? God decided. Instead of viewing this scene like a chess match between LIGHT and DARKNESS, view it as God making a clay pot.

Step 1: Gather the clay.

Step 2: Soften it up.

Step 3: Spin it on the wheel.

Step 4: Carefully shape it with your hands.

Step 5: Toss a log onto the fire.***

Step 6: Bake the clay pot.

Step 7: Let it cool.

This might be oversimplification, but Ramses is the LOG. God loves the clay pot that is humanity, and in taking a bit of dirt (Genesis), he carefully follows a plan that will result in something useful by the end of the process (Revelation). To make his dream happen, he needs a few logs.

Look at all the good guys who do evil (David, Paul, Ninevites.)

God wants them redeemed. Heck, what if he wants 99.9% of humanity redeemed. (here's my optimism). What if…it's only the PREDESTINED Sons of Perdition that are lost causes and he'll find the other lost sheep one way or another? Goats don't count?

In thought, word, and deed, Ramses the Great appears to oppose God, and even after going to the (ten)th degree, Ramses sticks with Belial. Yes, he's been conned, but perhaps he was destined to play the part of the log.

CHAPTER SEVEN

THE (G)REATEST (O)F (A)LL (T)IME.

I'll admit: those first three heads were "speculative." When John is told there were five heads that had already existed, we could be talking about the five previous Caesars. It's boring but quite possible. My problem is that I'm always seeking the most EPIC answer possible. To quote Fox Mulder, "I want to believe." It's just how I'm wired. I don't want tepid and realistic; I want grand and great.

Heck, there's no proof at all that connects John's 7 with Daniel's 4. I want it to be true. I don't think it's too much of a stretch that contained within the book of Daniel (which begins with End Times/Antichrist talk and ends with End Times/Antichrist talk) there are clues about the "many antichrists" previously alluded to. So now we're going to dive into Daniel and try to match up the clues given to real people. Unlike those obscure names like Lamech and Nimrod, my fourth name will be pretty famous.

Alexander the Great.

Oh, you've heard of him? You've seen the movie? Watched the mini-series? Historically, this guy is considered to be one of the greatest military minds to ever exist, which is certainly a trait worthy of cloning. In a short time, he created one of the largest empires of the era. He's literally the Greatest of All Time, the Goat.

Well, just like John was scratching his head when confronted with a seven headed dragon, it turns out it's not so hard to figure out the symbolism of Daniel 8. Remember, after all the layers of prophecy were given to John, the angel clearly explains that the dragon represented literal kings. Full stop. Guess what happens in Daniel 8. Layer, layer, layer...a literal king.

"The Shaggy Goat Represents the Kingdom of Greece"

It's that easy. The angel says so. Now before you get excited and start throwing out your favorite Greek kings like Leonidas or Constantine II, remember...there were other clues that needed to match. Another thing to remember is that this prophecy was given to Daniel in approximately 600 BC, so there's a lot of time to look it over. It might help to know the chapter, so here we go:

> **[Daniel 8:1] In the third year of the reign of king Belshazzar a vision appeared unto me, even unto me Daniel, after that which appeared unto me at the first. [2] <u>And I saw in a vision;</u> and it came to pass, when I saw, that I was at Shushan in the palace, which is in the province of Elam; and I saw in a vision, and I was by the river of Ulai. [3] Then I lifted up mine eyes, and saw, and, behold, there stood before the river <u>a ram which</u>**

<u>had two horns</u>: and the two horns were high; but one was higher than the other, and the higher came up last. [4] I saw the ram pushing westward, and northward, and southward; so that no beasts might stand before him, neither was there any that could deliver out of his hand; but he did according to his will, and became great.

[5] And as I was considering, behold, an <u>he goat came from the west</u> on the face of the whole earth, and touched not the ground: and the goat had a notable horn between his eyes. [6] And he came to the ram that had two horns, which I had seen standing before the river, and ran unto him in the fury of his power. [7] And I saw him come close unto the ram, and he was moved with choler against him, and smote the ram, and brake his two horns: and there was no power in the ram to stand before him, but he cast him down to the ground, and stamped upon him: and there was none that could deliver the ram out of his hand. [8] Therefore the he goat waxed very great: and when he was strong, the great horn was broken; and for it came up four notable ones toward the four winds of heaven. [9] And out of one of them came forth <u>a little horn</u>, which waxed exceeding great, toward the south, and toward the east, and toward the pleasant land. [10] And it waxed great, even to the host of heaven; and it cast down some of the host and of the stars to the ground, and stamped upon them. [11] Yea, he magnified himself even to the prince of the host, and by him <u>the daily sacrifice</u> was taken away, and the place of his sanctuary was cast down. [12] And an host was given him against the daily sacrifice by reason of transgression, and it cast down the truth to the ground; and it practiced, and prospered. [13] Then I heard one saint speaking, and another saint said unto that certain saint which spake, How long shall be the vision concerning the daily sacrifice, and the transgression of desolation, to give both the sanctuary and the

host to be trodden under foot? [14] And he said unto me, Unto two thousand and three hundred days; then shall the sanctuary be cleansed.

Before we get to the angel's explanation, let's just unpack a bit of what we just read. The first thing to note is that this is AFTER Nebuchadnezzar's dream of THE Antichrist.

Remember the scary Frankenstein DNA monster?

Daniel told him that his dream was about the fellow from the End Times. Since that day, Daniel likely has been pondering this future. Well, here he gets a few more clues about the End Times and Seal #5-6-7 which happen "about" three and a half years before the END.

Even though there are three beasts mentioned, I believe it is showing a "passage of time" and also previewing a few "anti-christs" at the same time. The historical prophecy is so impressive that many "critical" Biblical scholars assume Daniel was written after all this stuff had happened. Prophecy can't be this perfect, can it?

Let's look at what the angel said to Daniel.

[Daniel 8:15] And it came to pass, when I, even I Daniel, had seen the vision, and sought for the meaning, then, behold, there stood before me as the appearance of a man. [16] And I heard a man's voice between the banks of Ulai, which called, and said, Gabriel, make this man to understand the vision. [17] So he came near where I stood: and when he came, I was afraid, and fell upon my face: but he said unto me, Understand, O son of man: for at <u>the time of the end</u> shall be the vision. [18] Now as he was speaking with me, I was in a deep sleep on my face toward the ground: but he touched me, and set me upright. [19] And he said, Behold, I will make thee

know what shall be in the last end of the indignation: for at the time appointed the end shall be.[20] The ram which thou sawest having two horns are the kings of Media and Persia.[21] And the rough goat is the king of Grecia: and the great horn that is between his eyes is the first king. [22] Now that being broken, whereas four stood up for it, four kingdoms shall stand up out of the nation, but not in his power. [23] And in the latter time of their kingdom, when the transgressors are come to the full, a king of fierce countenance, and understanding dark sentences, shall stand up. [24] And his power shall be mighty, but not by his own power: and he shall destroy wonderfully, and shall prosper, and practice, and shall destroy the mighty and the holy people. [25] And through his policy also he shall cause craft to prosper in his hand; and he shall magnify himself in his heart, and by peace shall destroy many: he shall also stand up against the Prince of princes; but he shall be broken without hand. [26] And the vision of the evening and the morning which was told is true: wherefore shut thou up the vision; for it shall be for many days. [27] And I Daniel fainted, and was sick certain days; afterward I rose up, and did the king's business; and I was astonished at the vision, but none understood it.

As I said, this is about the End Times and also the coming events that will have a connection to it. With just this prophecy, you could certainly toss in the candidacy of any of several kings that ruled Babylon, Assyria, or Persia. Yet that's why I dismiss any of the "rams" from being connected to the Antichrists. The prophecy is just laying out some historical context so we know exactly who to look out for. Nebuchadnezzar, once again, is a big name and certainly could be an antichrist head, but considering that his story ends with him praising and honoring Daniel's God, um…now he's a good guy?

Problematic.

The same thing goes for Xerxes the Great of Persia. Yes, he conquers everything, but then there's the little problem of Queen Esther, who also seems to redeem this conquering heathen.

Problematic.

But the goat?

Historically, that one jumps right off the page. One Greek king conquers Persia (and then some). One Greek king dies young and then has his mighty empire divided up to his four generals. That's Alexander the Great!

It's only a few lines, and like the Ram, he could just be a bridge to the SERIOUS antichrist candidate, the Little Horn. We'll get to Antiochus Epiphanes in Chapter Eight, so we're done talking about him for now. Yet this Goat that's now on our radar gets another prophecy from Daniel, and for that reason, he's my guy.

It's All Greek to Me

Before we get to Alexander, let's look at some Biblical foreshadowing about Greece. I immersed myself in Greek Mythology at the same time I read several versions of the Bible, but it wasn't until I was an adult that I came across the next story. The reason for it is my NRSV Bible did not include a few books of the Bible that are found in the Catholic Bible.

Time for a rabbit hole.

While Martin Luther might've been right when he dismissed a few books because of their lack of prophecy or God insight (complain to him), they did give ME some really cool historical insight into Greece and Little Greece. With the Book of Maccabees insight into history, I suddenly found some missing pieces in my NRSV Bible that made a complete story.

Judges 19 contains a horrible story. Some scoffers claim the Bible was an invention, and if that's true, WHY WOULD YOU INCLUDE this story? This three-chapter anecdote involves gang rape and sodomy and THEN spirals into a nasty tribe-against-tribe civil war that leads to near tribal genocide. Rough stuff!

So why include it?

Tucked into the story is a strange answer.

First of all, "Benjamin" carried some bad connotations for me. Everyone remembers him as the cute littlest brother of Joseph who is taken as hostage to get all the bad brothers together for some reckoning. You remember, Joseph and the coat of many colors? Pit? Slavery? Fake death? Who did the convincing? Who poisoned the brothers against him? I don't know if it says, but look at the very end of Jacob/Israel's life. On his death bed, he gives some prophecy and closing statements about his twelve boys. While some sink and others swim, check out what he says about Benjamin's future:

[Genesis 49:27] Benjamin is a ravenous wolf: in the morning he shall devour the prey, and at night he shall divide the spoil.

And from that, folks associated with the tribe of Benjamin (Saul) are often villains despite their Hebrew ancestry. I bring this up because the bad guys in Judges 19-22 are...the Tribe of Benjamin. Yet that's lightweight when compared to the other description they get:

[Judges 19:22] certain sons of Belial.

Considering all the horrible things happening in this story, it's easy to ignore this reference, but considering how it connects back to Ramses the Great, the Golden Calf, and the Canaanites, it is an explanation on what corrupted this tribe.

The Benjaminite Sons of Belial put up an incredible fight. Despite overwhelming odds, the Children of Belial do not submit (hard hearted?) and it costs the alliance of "good guys" quite a bit to exterminate these rebels. Well, they don't exterminate them because of…prophecy reasons. So they let some of them live. The Tribe of Benjamin was spared.

While most ended up living in the shadows of mighty Judah (Judea), apparently, some of the survivors held a grudge and decided to leave Israel for a new start. This is where the Maccabees come into play with some tidbits that escaped my Lutheran upbringing.

1 Maccabees 12:21 "It is found in writing, that the Spartans and Jews are brethren, and that they are of the stock of Abraham"

Now, if you know anything about Spartan culture, it revolutionized the Greek tribes because of it s unique fighting style. Hold on…is that verse implying the Spartans were taught to fight by the Benjamites? The whole Goat=Greece thing was not invented by Daniel. In fact, it came from the era of Moses.

A "concept" or "god" known as Azazel was created. According to Hebrew lore, Azazel was a fallen angel who introduced secret knowledge to humans before the flood. You remember that chapter, the Empire of Lamech? A thousand years later, this secret knowledge (evil stuff) is still around, so to purge it from the ranks, a sacrifice is made.

[Leviticus 16:26]: And he that let go the goat for the scapegoat (Azazel) shall wash his clothes, and bathe his flesh in water, and afterward come into the camp.

The whole chapter is dedicated to the purging of evil with the goat sacrifice. Goat=Evil=Belial?

Time for speculation.

So if the Tribe of Benjamin turned to evil. And their evil is described as Belial. And the Spartans have connections to the Jews. And the symbol given to Greece is a goat. Dang! Alexander the Great is leading another army of Belial. The symbol for Arcadia is the goat god Pan or Faunus. The religion and worship of Pan was "foreign" to the other regions of Greece, but since Arcadia was such crappy land, these "foreigners" thrived in a region ignored by the Greeks.

Goats are baaaadd.

[Matthew 25:31] When the Son of man shall come in his glory, and all the holy angels with him, then shall he sit upon the throne of his glory: [32] And before him shall be gathered all nations: and he shall separate them one from another, as a shepherd divideth his sheep from the goats: [33] And he shall set the sheep on his right hand, but the goats on the left.

So when Daniel is warned by the angel that the Goat is coming, he likely knows what the implication means.

Of course, not all goats are bad, and the same applies for the tribe of Benjamin. Shortly after Daniel wrote his book, we get Esther. In that story, Mordecai is a Benjaminite and he was a good guy. Okay, so he did kinda pimp Esther, but he also supported her all the way to the throne of Persia. Outside of the tale of Esther, remember that her husband Xerxes does something quite curious: he invades Greece. There he clashes with the Spartans, and if not for some bad luck, would've destroyed Sparta. His failure opened the door to Alexander the Great.

Alexander By the Book

The stories of Alexander range from truthful historical accounts to folklore and invention. Each "expert" spins his textbook in a unique way, so I'm not sure how much of this next section is accurate. I'm not making it up, but I don't necessarily trust each and every source. When I read/heard something interesting, I jotted it down in my journal.

So after Alexander's father was killed (by Persians), he advanced his father's plans and rallied all of Greece to invade and defeat Persia. Along the way, he ended up fulfilling two Biblical prophecies. First, he sacked the island nation of Tyre, patiently building a causeway to defeat the immovable object that stood in his way. A bit later, he conquered Egypt. About this same time, he went out of his way to go to Jerusalem.

But not to tear it all down.

You see, Alexander had dreams of an "old man" for years. Knowing that Alexander's Army acted like bulldozers to any nation that opposed them, Israel quickly bent the knee and surrendered. When Alexander struts into Jerusalem, he stops in his tracks. The old man? Well, turns out the High Priest is the figure from his dreams. This is also where Alexander identifies himself as "the Goat" from Daniel's prophecy and spins it like the conquest is divine. Surprisingly, he does little to disrupt Israel. Yet he also implements a very subtle social plan that will change Israel. The language changes. The social norms change.

Even religion changes as the old school Pharisees give way to the woke Sadducees. Long after Alexander dies, his social systems continue to change the world and Israel.

The Occult History

Having studied mythology, there is a VERY complicated family tree that comes out of the story of the Odyssey involving the House of Tantalus (Menelaus), the House of Achilles, and the House of Odysseus. So when Philip of Macedon married Olympias, he not only united Greece but he also united a whole bunch of mythology. Greek mythology effectively ended with Odysseus returning home, but for Olympias, that era stayed alive through family trees. She was the perfect queen for the united King of Greece because of her bloodlines. Her father—named after the son of Achilles. Her beauty—yep, she was descended from Helen of Sparta.

Olympias had connections to strange mystery cults connected with orgiastic celebrations that involved sleeping in beds filled with snakes. Fun? Although she marries King Philip, it's not a very happy marriage. They did have a daughter together, who she named Cleopatra (not her, but still worthy of note), but with Alexander, even the conception got messy. Instead of boldly declaring Alexander as the rightful heir, she does something strange: she claims Zeus impregnated her with a thunderbolt prior to her marriage to Philip. Huh? Even Philip has strange dreams about his kid (pun intended) having connections to a lion. The day of his birth? Even stranger. There was a "good omen" involving a horse race at the Olympic games, but at the same time, there was a "bad omen" when the Temple of Artemis in Ephesus (One of the 7 Wonders of the World) was destroyed by fire.

A few years later, when Alexander was older, his sister Cleopatra was given in marriage to an uncle so Philip could consolidate power. At this wedding, Philip was killed by his own bodyguards. Even though Olympias wasn't there, many believed she gave the order. She seized power for her son, and Alexander the Great became king of Greece.

Born with one blue eye and one dark eye, Alexander the Great wasted little time and quickly invaded Persia, who received the blame for his father's assassination. On the way, he conquered many nations, including Egypt. He went deep into Egypt, seeking validation for his origins, and declared himself to be divine, mashing up Egyptian and Greek mythology to dub himself Ammon-Zeus with a label of "King of Kings."

Along with the omens involving Tyre and the Temple of Jerusalem, Alexander the Great faced the Gordian Knot, a big ball of knots that no one could figure out how to untangle. When faced with the challenge, Alexander offered an obvious solution. He took out his sword and cut the stupid thing in half—solving the riddle.

His goal remained on conquering Persia, but his primary focus remained ancient Babylon. After all, the symbol of ancient Babylon was the winged lion, so Alexander saw it as some sort of birthright or destiny to sit upon that ancient throne. Upsetting his Greek buddies, he made his new home at Babylon.

Historians claim that Alexander's "personal" god (not including himself) was the worship of Athena. Now in Greek and Roman (Minerva) mythology, Athena was a goddess of wisdom and a virgin. Yet she was also the Goddess of War, specifically organized warfare, which Alexander's forces excelled at. I bring this up because Athena appears to be a retelling of…Anath.

So Alexander the Great begins to connect to Babylon, where Nimrod and Semiramis once lived. Semiramis worship evolved into Anath worship, and Anath worship evolved into Athena worship. Beyond that thread, remember what I said about Menelaus (red head) landing in Egypt following the Trojan War. He was a Spartan. Ramses the Great? Red head. The Benjaminites? Sparta. Do you see all of the genetic connections happening beyond the occult stuff?

Even though Alexander the Great could've rested on his laurels (literally), he wasted no time before leading the army east. What led him east? We'll get to that later. Unlike other conquerors, he had a sophisticated plan—indoctrination. He rebuilt conquered lands, created a new city named Alexandria, and then created schools to reshape the new nation in his vision. It was highly influential, and long after his death, his policies remained.

That's a prime candidate for being an Antichrist.

Beyond the Goat

Of course, there's more to identifying the Antichrist, and as cool as Daniel 8's Goat prophecy, there is also the prophecy of Daniel 7. Unlike the Book of Revelation, Daniel is a collection of dreams. Most connect to the End Times theme. So Daniel 7 is a dream of "Four Beasts." Just like with John's Beast from Water, these beasts also come from water. Unfortunately, this dream is super symbolic and can be much more open to interpretation than the other dream in Daniel 8. Yet here's a quick synopsis

Four beasts come out of the sea

The first is a lion with eagle wings.

The second is a bear.

The third is a leopard.

The fourth is a four-headed thing.

The fourth has 10 horns.

A little horn comes next.

The Ancient of Days shows up.

Judgment Day arrives.

The beast is thrown into fire.

The Son of Man then rules forever and ever.

That's Daniel 8 in a nutshell. The last few bullets obviously show connections to John's Book of Revelation. Hey, it's a happy ending also. However, if you back this thing up from the End Times to Daniel back in 600ish BC, and then compare it to John 5+1+1=8, you realize a few clues.

John's 8th Beast is likely that "little horn" that comes from Daniel's 4th Beast.

The 10 horns of Beast #4 are likely the same 10 horns for John's Antichrist.

Yet if Daniel sees four beasts in his future, that supports my notion that the previous 3 beasts/heads/kings described by John as being in the past are also in Daniel's past. Conversely, Daniel's four beasts are likely John's 2+1+1=4.

Translation: 2 beasts will come between Daniel and John.

1 beast will come during John's life.

1 beast will come after John's 95 AD prophecy (Close to the End Times).

With Daniel's other prophecy in Chapter 8 predicting Alexander and Antiochus Epiphanes, I'm going to build the argument that the LION prophecy is also predicting Alexander. So let's take a close look at the language of it:

> **[Daniel 7:3] And four great beasts came up from the sea, diverse one from another. [4] The first was like <u>a lion</u>, and had <u>eagle's wings</u>: I beheld till the wings thereof were plucked, and it was <u>lifted up</u> from the earth, and made stand upon the feet as a man, and a man's <u>heart</u> was given to it.**

Thanks to papa Philip of Macedon, I have reason to get excited about the omen of Alexander's birth. That lion prophecy not only was viewed by Daniel but also by Alexander the Great's father. Kinda cool. The Eagle wings? Come on! Ancient Babylon is famous for its winged lion, isn't it? Now remember, both Greece and Babylon describe monsters, and how are these monsters known? They are genetic Frankensteins! Mess with nature and you get monsters. But that's another rabbit hole.

Obviously, a heart that is lifted up could be code for arrogance. Was Alexander arrogant? Oh yeah, baby. He was still a kid (bad pun) when his father died. Heck, he might've helped mom secure his own throne. So verse 4 might be identifying Alexander having to grow up and rule an empire as a young man, which he did. Yet the book of Maccabees has another fascinating verse that offers insight. (come on, Martin!)

> **1 Macc 1:1 "And it happened, after that Alexander son of Philip, the Macedonian, who came out of the land of Chettiim, had smitten Darius king of the Persians and Medes, that he**

reigned in his stead, the first over Greece, 2 And made many wars, and won many strong holds, and slew the kings of the earth, 3 And went through to the ends of the earth, and took spoils of many nations, insomuch that the earth was quiet before him; whereupon he was exalted and his heart was lifted up."

See?

It's not just Jason Lee Willis speculating. Here is a great connection for Alexander the Great and the Daniel 7 prophecy.

Beyond Babylon

That was probably enough on Alexander the Great. Daniel warned. Alexander fulfilled. The young conqueror did his thing and died.

Oh, but there is so much more.

So bear with me.

Remember the House of the Raised Head in the Nimrod chapter? Well, when Alexander the Great did take control of Babylon, the restoration of this ancient site became one of his first important projects. If he'd lived, what were his goals? Dang…

As it turns out, when Alexander returned from his trip to India, he didn't last long. History scholars all have theories, so your FACTS depend on who you listen to. Remember that Alexander's four generals get the king to fulfill the **"four kingdoms shall stand up out of the nation"** prophecy. Cassander is high on the list for being the poisoner. Once Alexander died, he went out of his way to obliterate the Esagila project. Any good archeology found…gone! Then Cassander has Olympias and Alexander's sons killed. Poof! Gone! Nasty guy, but if Alexander the Great is full-fledged Eeeviiil, then is he doing something positive?

Alexander's fire burns out so quickly that folks kinda forget what he was trying to accomplish in the first place. No sooner had he conquered the Mediterranean than he set his sights on: India?

Whoa…why?

Cuz? Just cuz?

Remember that Alexander seems to know his dark mythology. He knows antiquity. So in conquering Media, Ariana, and Bactria he certainly had to have had a goal, right? I can only speculate, but in trying to conquer Sogdiana, in the north, it appears like he is trying to go up and around the Himalayas into…

    A. The Taklimakan Desert?

    B. The Gobi Desert?

    C. China?

    D. Tibet?

If he'd won, he would've been able to pass into eastern Asia and right into a couple of nasty deserts, so A & B seem unlikely. Even if you picked China, he could've gotten there by staying south and going through India (which he later did). So if China was his goal, he didn't act like it. Instead, he loses momentum and men by trying to get on the northern side of the Himalayas. So what's in Tibet?

The Navel of the Universe!

Militarily, there is little significance, but spiritually and mythologically, one of the most important mountains on the planet would have been in his grasp. Today, it is known as Mount

Kailash, and while not as high as Mount Everest, it is revered by four major religions as some sort of Eden. Why? Well, four rivers begin there. While not the Tigris, Euphrates Gihon, and Pishon, it's still the mother of other major Asian rivers. Plus, the lore behind it is that it is an ancient place where gods once dwelt and acts of creation and destruction occurred.

See?

Big Al would've been intrigued by such a place.

While he failed, another of my candidates for being an antichrist head succeeded in going there. Well, he didn't go. He was smarter than Alexander. Rather than bringing the entire German army, he just sent a team of researchers to Tibet where Mount Kailash is also known as the Nine-Story Swastika Mountain. We'll talk about our German friends later.

So now you see why I was interested in Big Al's motivations to go in this general direction. History leaves a few fascinating clues. While the Battle of Jaxartes isn't technically a loss for Alexander, he turns around and decides to begin his campaign into India. Was he trying to reach Mount Kailash by the Himalayan pass? Maybe.

In the Alexander legends, he leaves behind a gate. Apparently he creates a gate made of Adamantine (sounds like Marvel) to keep the evil army he'd just faced from ever coming south to mess with his new empire. Huh? Oh yes, this legend has a dozen different versions with a dozen different twists.

Who was he trying to keep out?

Gog and Magog

Now some of those ancient interpretations have this literally translate into the Goths and Magoths, which is cool. In fact, I used this in my novel series. Sure enough, two types of goths rise up and cause havoc throughout Europe and history. Heck, Goths even sack Rome and haul off the wealth of an empire. I even followed the East Goths (visigoths) and West Goths (ostrogoths) as they settled in the Mountains of Transylvania. It's cool stuff.

But Biblically, Gog and Magog open up a whole can of worms.

The Armies of Gog and Magog

The first time this name is used in the Bible is that huge nation list found in Genesis 10. Magog is listed as one of the sons of Japheth. Since Japheth is one of Noah's three sons, he is often credited as being the father of the European people—the people of the north. 1 Chronicles 1:5 echoes this same fact that Magog is a son of Japheth. So far, this is boring stuff, right. Well, it gets way more interesting when you flip to the back of the book and find these two names in the Book of Revelation:

> **[Revelation 20:7] And when the thousand years are expired, Satan shall be loosed out of his prison, [8]And shall go out to deceive the nations which are in the four quarters of the earth, Gog and Magog, to gather them together to battle: the number of whom is as the sand of the sea. [9] And they went up on the breadth of the earth, and compassed the camp of the saints about, and the beloved city: and fire came down from God out of heaven, and devoured them. [10] And the devil that deceived them was cast into the lake of fire and brimstone, where the beast and the false prophet are, and shall be tormented day and night for ever and ever.**

Whoa…So the Army of Satan will include Gog and Magog? No wonder Alexander built a gate! So an ancient people will rise up in the future and help Satan try to kill Jesus and Company in a big battle at least a thousand years following the reign of the Antichrist. Wow. So who are these guys that help Satan fight against Jesus and his 144,000?

The first problem we have is that in the timeline of the prophecies, this is one of the last things to happen. We get earthquakes, disasters, ecological nightmares, Apollyon and his monsters, and then…the Battle of Armageddon, which has the Antichrist and his Prophet being thrown into a newly created Lake of Fire. Oh, and for humans on earth? We get 75 pound hailstones and a "sword" from Jesus's mouth cleansing the earth of any and all life. All this happens BEFORE this Gog and Magog incident. So what are our options?

Option A: Jesus missed some.

Option B: The 144,000 go bad after 1,000 years.

Option C: They are not "human."

Option D: They were not "home" on Earth

All four options spark the imagination and are also problematic. So any theories on Gog and Magog should be taken lightly (even from me). Simply put, it's pretty hard to "call this" one.

I say this because for thousands of years, folks have made theories about who these people are. Is it a genetic thing? Not clear. Is it a religious thing? Not clear. So when you find theories on the internet this is how diverse your answers will be: Sythians, Hazars, Huns, Mongols, "red" Jews, Amazons, 10 Lost Tribes, Turks, Goths (told ya), Napoleon, Germany, Russia, China,

Communists, and as George Bush once claimed…Weapons of Mass Destruction. Folks toss this term around freely.

We'll come back to Gog and Magog again when I talk about Mount Kailash, the Swastika, and another prophecy involving the Jews vs. Gog and Magog.

I want to close by bringing up this point: Team Antichrist seems aware of their own prophecies. Alexander went to Egypt…Ramses the Great. Alexander went to Babylon…Nimrod. Alexander went to Jerusalem…End Times. Then he goes hauling off to the East, where he fails yet builds a gate to keep the prophecy of Gog and Magog from happening. Antichrists will be so self-centered and selfish that they will want to preserve their life and rule for as long as they can. They don't want the End Times. They want to DELAY it to prolong their rule.

The GOAT died young, and from his mighty empire…four kingdoms.

One of those guys takes hating God and the Jews to a whole other level.

CHAPTER EIGHT

CROSSING THE LINE

It's not too often that Jesus is wrong. If you crank the "God Dial" all the way down to zero, he was still a fellow who seemed to know the scriptures better than any living Pharisee. He could toss out textual support and prophecy at any moment. Even as a twelve-year-old boy, he wowed the crowd in the temple. Even the most jaded Pharisee would admit: He knows his stuff.

The disciples must've seen this same ability, yet they also were able to see that "God dial" on display quite often over those three years of ministry. The Word of God could speak things into existence. These fellows saw him talk the talk and then also walk the walk. Yet he did come down to earth in human form, so I guess that diminished form must've made the disciples complacent about his divinity from time to time. Looking back on their time with Christ, they finally saw the big picture. They trusted. They believed.

Now, thousands of years later, we also have the perspective of Jesus being perfect. He was the unblemished lamb that died without sin. He was the infallible Son of God as part of the Holy Trinity.

But by the time he got to Easter week, Jesus was pretty tired, which explains his mistake.

Not buying it?

Jesus doesn't make mistakes, right?

So in a contest between scholars and Jesus, you should always side with...Jesus!

Good.

Now that we're all on the same page, it's time to bring up something strange and quite subtle that Jesus said.

Matthew, Mark, and Luke all record a very detailed End Times conversation that began with Jesus talking about the destruction of the temple (and earth) and then later that night, either James, John, Peter, or Andrew asked him "When will these things be?"

And Jesus goes on to drop a ton of prophecy on them. John never bothered to write this moment into his Gospel since he'd already written the Book of Revelation and included the Apostasy, the Red Horse, the Pale Horse, the 5th Seal, the 1st Seal, the 6th Seal, as well as talk about the Antichrist. He goes into great detail about the signs of the "Final Countdown," a quick reference to "some" of the current generation "not dying" until this happens, and when it does happen, it'll be pretty quick. But hey, don't worry you four—you've got a whole planet that needs evangelizing first.

It was a pretty heavy moment for those four disciples and also for most Christians.

Just like Daniel, 1 of the 4 disciples wanted to know WHEN it would happen.

(It's complicated apparently).

Yet when explaining himself and the "triggers" that will signal the End Times and that final countdown, Jesus brings up a fulfilled prophecy.

Hold on.

A fulfilled prophecy?

If a prophecy has been fulfilled, then how is it a prophecy?

Remember, Jesus isn't wrong.

Our interpretation is wrong.

What am I talking about?

Here is Mark's account of the moment:

[Mark13:9] So be on your guard. You will be handed over to the councils and beaten in the synagogues. On My account, you will stand before governors and kings as witnesses to them. [10] And <u>the gospel must first be proclaimed</u> to all the nations. [11] But when they arrest you and hand you over, do not worry beforehand what to say. Instead, speak whatever you are given at that time, for it will not be you speaking, but the Holy Spirit. [12] Brother will betray brother to death, and a father his child. Children will rise against their parents and have them put to death. [13] You will be hated by everyone on account of My name, but the one who perseveres to the end will be saved. [14] So when you see the <u>abomination of desolation</u> standing where it should not be <u>(let the reader understand)</u>, then let those who are in Judea flee to the mountains. [15] Let no one on the housetop go back inside to retrieve anything from his house. [16] And let no one in the field return for his cloak.

[17] How miserable those days will be for pregnant and nursing mothers! **[18]** Pray that it will not occur in the winter. **[19]** For in those days there will be tribulation unmatched from the beginning of God's creation until now, and never to be seen again. **[20]** If the Lord had not shortened those days, nobody would be saved. But for the sake of the elect, whom He has chosen, He has shortened them.

[21] At that time if anyone says to you, 'Look, here is the Christ!' or 'There He is!' do not believe it. **[22]** For false Christs and false prophets will appear and perform signs and wonders that would deceive even the elect, if that were possible. **[23]** So be on your guard; I have told you everything in advance.

Again, the question was asked. When's this going to happen? Jesus casually previews two thousand years of Christianity spreading to the nations as the first condition of the return. He then gives some very "it'll be bad" characterizations before dropping a super specific clue:

The Abomination of Desolation.

Hold, we've heard that phrase before.

Oh yeah, Daniel mentioned it also.

After Daniel nailed the prophecy about Alexander the Great showing up, folks flipped to the next prophecy for insight. Sure enough, after Alexander died, his empire broke up into 4 lesser kingdoms, and from one of those kingdoms, a villain known as Antiochus Epiphanes showed up to torment the Jews.

Daniel called it.

And Jesus called out the interpretation as being...WRONG! He even had his dramatic aside comment: "(let the reader understand)." Being the super scholar, Jesus knew the Pharisees were wrong about a bunch of stuff, so when he's explaining the End Times to his four guys, he brings up the AofD prophecy NOT as being a prophecy about Antiochus Epiphanes but as a prophecy that will signal the End Times arrival.

"So when you see the abomination of desolation standing..."

That's our clue, folks.

Yo John, you awake? Jesus just gave us THE CLUE about when the End Times will start the final countdown.

(Let the Reader Understand):

In a nutshell, Jews looked back at a great conflict between the Maccabees and the Assyrian King known as Antiochus Epiphanes and felt that he fulfilled Daniel's prophecy.

Which he did.

But there were several prophecies.

Remember Nebuchadnezzar's Frankenstein monster? Antiochus Epiphanes likely was part of that metal monster.

Remember Daniel's vision of the four coming beasts? Antiochus Epiphanes likely was the bear with three ribs in its mouth.

And the Goat prophecy? Antiochus Epiphanes was almost certainly the little horn (the dude was evil). Heck, I'm writing this whole chapter about how he's one of the antichrist heads, so he lit up that spiritual radar back in the day. But in the Goat prophecy, there is a phrase that gets used 3 times in the Book of Daniel.

Here's the first:

[Daniel 8:9] And out of one of them came forth a little horn, which waxed exceeding great, toward the south, and toward

the east, and toward the pleasant land. [10] And it waxed great, even to the host of heaven; and it cast down some of the host and of the stars to the ground, and stamped upon them. [11] Yea, he magnified himself even to the prince of the host, and by him the daily sacrifice was taken away, and the place of his sanctuary was cast down. [12] And an host was given him against the daily sacrifice by reason of transgression, and it cast down the truth to the ground; and it practiced, and prospered. [13] Then I heard one saint speaking, and another saint said unto that certain saint which spake, How long shall be the vision concerning <u>the daily sacrifice</u>, and <u>the transgression of desolation</u>, to give both the sanctuary and the host to be trodden under foot? [14] And he said unto me, Unto two thousand and three hundred days; then shall the sanctuary be cleansed.

We'll break down the details in this passage in a bit, but I'm cool with it matching up with the real Antiochus Epiphanes. Daily sacrifice? Yep. Desolation? Yep. Hold those thoughts. Notice the question asked here: How long shall we (the Jews) be afflicted by this loser? The answer is given: 2,300. When Antiochus goes to war with the Maccabee Jews, this is the length of time. It works. Happy Hanukkah. Unfortunately, there are two other passages that bring up the Abomination of Desolation.

Here's the second:

[Daniel 11:30] For the ships of Chittim shall come against him: therefore he shall be grieved, and return, and have indignation against the holy covenant: so shall he do; he shall even return, and have intelligence with them that forsake the holy covenant. [31] And arms shall stand on his part, and they shall pollute the sanctuary of strength, and shall take away <u>the daily sacrifice</u>, and <u>they shall place the abomination that maketh</u>

<u>desolate</u>. [32] And such as do wickedly against the covenant shall he corrupt by flatteries: but the people that do know their God shall be strong, and do exploits. [33] And they that understand among the people shall instruct many: yet they shall fall by the sword, and by flame, by captivity, and by spoil, many days. [34] Now when they shall fall, they shall be holpen with a little help: but many shall cleave to them with flatteries. [35] And some of them of understanding shall fall, to try them, and to purge, and to make them white, even to the time of the end: because it is yet for a time appointed.

[36] And the king shall do according to his will; and he shall exalt himself, and magnify himself above every god, and shall speak marvellous things against the God of gods, and shall prosper till the indignation be accomplished: for that that is determined shall be done. [37] Neither shall he regard the God of his fathers, nor the desire of women, nor regard any god: for he shall magnify himself above all. [38] But in his estate shall he honor the God of forces: and a god whom his fathers knew not shall he honor with gold, and silver, and with precious stones, and pleasant things. [39] Thus shall he do in the most strongholds with a strange god, whom he shall acknowledge and increase with glory: and he shall cause them to rule over many, and shall divide the land for gain.

This one might not be Antiochus. It could be, but it also could be more of the final battle described in the End Times. Yet it does bring up our two phrases: sacrifice and abomination.

Here's the third one:

[Daniel 12:8] And I heard, but I understood not: then said I, O my Lord, what <u>shall be the end</u> of these things? [9]And he said, Go thy way, Daniel: for the words are closed up and sealed till the time of the end. [10] Many shall be purified, and made white, and tried; but the wicked shall do wickedly: and none of

the wicked shall understand; but <u>the wise shall understand</u>. 11 And from the time that the <u>daily sacrifice</u> shall be taken away, and the <u>abomination that maketh desolate</u> set up, there shall be <u>a thousand two hundred and ninety days</u>. [12] Blessed is he that waiteth, and cometh to the thousand three hundred and five and thirty days. [13] But go thou thy way till the end be: for thou shalt rest, and stand in thy lot at the end of the days.

This passage is fun. Daniel asks a bold question (different than his earlier question). This time, he clears his throat and asks about the End Times. Not what's next. Not who's next. Not how long we have left. He jumps to the End Times and wants to know the clue that will identify the beginning of the End Times. His answer: The Daily Sacrifice will stop (&) the Abomination of Desolation is set up. When THAT happens, you'll have 1,290 days. Dang, that's only 3 ½ years!

Got it?

Let's get back to Jesus.

When 1 of the 4 disciples asks Jesus about the End Times, Jesus brings up the Abomination of Desolation. Why? It's the trigger. When the AofD appears, the final days have arrived. Tick, tick, tick…boom!

Jesus knows this is a complicated prophecy because he says it is: **(let the reader understand).** Yet when you look at the Daniel 12 prophecy, it states that the End Times will come 1,290 days after 1) Daily Sacrifice is ended and 2) the Abomination of Desolation goes "muh, ha, ha." The world did not end after Antiochus Epiphanes destroyed the temple and set up his own altar.

What does this mean?

It's still an unfulfilled prophecy.

The Pharisees/Scholars were/are wrong.

Yes, Antiochus did some stuff. Bad stuff. Yes, he messed with the Temple. But according to Jesus, this is the prophecy that will signal the End Times. So we need new definitions for our wrong interpretation of the Daily Sacrifice and Abomination of Desolation. If we're looking for the wrong things, we'll never notice the end times.

The Historical Antiochus Epiphanes

We know quite a bit about this guy since he was born during the era of historians. Now, I'm paraphrasing a summary, so if you want the gritty details, go read it. Following the death of Alexander the Great, his empire was given to his four generals:

Ptolemy: who ruled Egypt.

Cassander: who ruled old Macedon/Greece.

Antigonus: who ruled Turkey.

Seleucus: Who ruled Assyria and the west.

That's how it started, and two centuries later, Antiochus Epiphanes IV finds himself in charge of the Seleucid Empire. Yet even his birth has villainous tones.

First, he was born with the name Mithradates. He took the name Antiochus Epiphanes later in life, which means "God Manifest." Yep, that's a big ego. Check. Back in those days, folks played around with the syllables and turned his name into a phrase that meant "The Mad One." That's telling. Yet Mithradates? You see, that is a very complicated name. Today, historians claim Mithraism is a "mystery" religion (vs. a public religion) which is proven by the secret caves and underground shrines centered around Rome. The Roman version of this mystery religion is often credited with the rites and levels of one of the first secret societies. Yet the origins of the religion have connections to Zoroastrianism.

Zoroaster?

Yep, I last mentioned him when I talked about the religious origins of Nimrod (Head #2). You see, just like Zoroaster, Mithras came from Persia (Iran). According to archeologists, there is a common theme of bull-slaying.

When did I last mention bulls? Oh yes, Baal's symbol. (see Golden Calf). So Mithras is checking off a lot of boxes, isn't it? Mithras tradition holds that he was born from a rock in most origin stories yet he also has connections to a water god (beast from earth? Beast from water?). His visual iconography is a fun mixture of images: part man, serpent tail, lion head, wings while holding a caduceus (Hermes/Mercury).

Oh, and a fun coincidence? Mithradates was born on...December 25th. Oh boy, does this detail send scoffers and scholars into a tizzy. Me? I'm not afraid of this fact. In my **Examining Christmas** study, I wrote a whole chapter on the support for Jesus being born on December 25th, but just because TWO figures had the same birthday doesn't mean you can throw the baby out with the bath water (probably a bad metaphor to use). Instead of taking away from Jesus, I think this is adding to the evil mystique of our villain. We'll get back to the importance of this birthday in a bit.

So after being born in 215 BC, little Mithradates officially became the king of the Seleucid Kingdom at the age of 40 as Antiochus Epiphanes. (Died in 164 BC). Early in his life, he was kept as a political prisoner in Rome. Even though he was "mad" and saw himself as a god, historians record that he liked to hang out with the commoners. While his empire wasn't massive, he did stir the pot a bit. Our "bear" managed to eat a few "ribs" once he was in power. In 170 BC, he invaded Egypt, displacing Ptolemy VI, who became a puppet king who ruled from Rome. In 168 BC, he attacked Cyprus. Around this time, he got the attention of Rome and in a dramatic moment that saw the rise and fall of two empires, Roman Gaius Laenas literally drew a line in the sand and told Antiochus Epiphanes enough is enough.

So Antiochus Epiphanes stopped messing with Roman allies and instead turned to Israel. As the southern neighbor to Assyria/Seleucid Empire, Israel had heard rumors that Antiochus Epiphanes had died in battle and took advantage of this. (They deposed the High Priest Menelaus and replaced him with their own guy, Jason). Oh, boy. AE did not like this. So in 167, Antiochus attacked Israel, restored Menelaus, and executed anybody and everybody associated with this little coup. Historians describe AE as "raging like a wild animal" as they massacred 80,000 Jews in 3 days (Hitler sighs from his room in hell).

Remember, Israel has been part of Alexander's system for two centuries now, and Hellenized Jews are now prevalent. AE outlawed traditional rites and promoted the Greek/Roman worship of Zeus (not a mystery religion). In retaking Jerusalem, women were forced to throw circumcised babies from the walls and much of the restoration to Jerusalem was destroyed.

Hammer Time

The Maccabean Revolt of 167-160 BC covers the story of a Jewish man named Mathathias and his guerilla war against the enemies of God. For modern Jews, it is a familiar tale that brought an important holiday: Hanukkah. Despite deaths and major setbacks, this guy (known as "the Hammer") outlasts Antiochus Epiphanes and helps Israel gain independence in 142 BC (although the Hasmoneans bring King Herod later). At the center of this David vs. Goliath 2.0 is the miracles of lights, where they restore the Temple and witness a miraculous loaves and fishes moment involving the oil.

Oh, that happened in late December. Apparently, AE wanted to celebrate his birthday on the 25th (2 Mac 6.7) and desecrate the temple. How? He decided to insult the Jews by involving a pig (Leviticus 11, ew) and also plant a statue of Zeus. And yada, yada, yada, the Maccabees take the temple back (on December 25th) and celebrate this cleaning of the temple in the Feast of Dedication (1 Mac 4.52) each December (Chislev/Kislev).

Never heard of this story? Well, due to some anti-Semitism and heavy-handed editorialism, most modern Protestant Bibles don't include this section. Why? Martin Luther, when translating Latin into German, noted that they were simply historical books. No prophecies, angels, or God commands within it. So, he left it out. Yet it's a cool read. It begins with Alexander the Great's "his heart was lifted up" invasion. It records battle by battle details (kinda boring). Mentions that Spartans have Jewish lineage. Brings up that time Rome helped. Adds details about Jeremiah and the hiding of the Ark. Has graphic scenes of torture and brutality that made it very rated R. Oh, and it furthers my argument about Baal and Anath and their continued worship under new names. So I found it quite interesting.

Ultimately, it chronicles how Antiochus Epiphanes departed to death with a Parthian problem in Armenia. During this battle, AE dies suddenly in 164 BC. Suddenly, it explains how he was divinely killed by "worms and ulcers." Gross. No more AE. Following this death, Parthia becomes a global power and opposes another rising power in Rome.

That's the "Biblical" story of Antiochus Epiphanes vs. the Hammer.

Matching the Prophecy

At the beginning of this chapter, I theorized how Antiochus Epiphanes MOSTLY matched the Daniel 8 prophecy.

Little Horn=Antiochus Epiphanes

Waxed Great= war

South=Egypt

East=Parthia

Pleasant Land=Judea

Host of Heaven=??? (we'll get back to that one)

To the Ground=Razing Jerusalem

Magnified Himself=Declared himself a god

Even to the Prince of the Host=??? (we'll get back to that one)

Daily Sacrifice=when AE redecorated the temple.

Host=the Maccabean Revolt

2300=The revolt lasted 7 years.

Broken without Hand=that's AE's sudden illness.

That, folks, is a very, very impressive prophecy. Because of the accuracy of predicting Antiochus Epiphanes and his vile genocidal war against the Jews, folks tossed all the prophecies in Daniel and ascribed them to AE. Yet when Jesus showed up two centuries later, he has to correct his disciples that this was an unfulfilled prophecy.

So some of the most popular theories about the Antichrist involve him doing the same stuff as AE. The "trigger" will be: temple…pig…Zeus…Jerusalem.

I've read fictional accounts of the Antichrist that have him literally riding a pig through the temple in Jerusalem. The problem? There's no temple. So since 1948 when the word Palestine was erased from the map and replaced with Israel, American politicians have been doing all they can to help aid the Jews in rebuilding the Temple. Yet to do that, they'll need to rid Israel of all the Muslims who rebuilt their own temple on the foundation of the old temple.

Yet I think Jesus purposefully cautioned us/disciples that the interpretation of this prophecy is a bit off. Remember, he established "Abomination of Desolation" and "Daily Sacrifice" as the two triggers to count down the literal days to the end. The World Will End in 1,290 Days (Dan 12).

Yet nothing happened!

So what does that mean?

Re-defining Daily Sacrifice

You know what they say about assumptions, right? From Judas Maccabeus to Judas Iscariot, most Jews ascribed the prophecies of Daniel to ALL fit Antiochus Epiphanes. Yet according to the wording, once the Daily Sacrifice was ended, the world was supposed to come to an end 1,290 days later. The assumption was that the Daily Sacrifice was happening in the Temple. There are a lot of IF's in this theory.

If the Abomination of Desolation means (A) Zeus or (B) pigs…maybe.

If the Temple is the one built by Solomon…(destroyed).

If the Temple is the one rebuilt by Nehemiah and Company…(destroyed).

If the Temple is the one rebuilt by Herod…(destroyed).

If Daily Sacrifice is the High Priests making offerings in the Holiest of Holies…problem.

The problem? Well, all of the temples built in Jerusalem have been torn down at some point. The Daily Sacrifice by High Priests has been stopped on multiple occasions. The Babylonians did it. Antiochus Epiphanes did it. The Romans did it many times. I don't think it has anything to do with Jewish priests or the Temple of Jerusalem.

After all, Jesus corrected his guys when he told them that this prophecy was still connected to the End Times. So stop expecting a rebuilt temple. Stop picturing an Antichrist figure riding a pig through the temple. Sure, the Antichrist might repeat many of the same things that Antiochus Epiphanes did back in the day, but we might miss it if we're not paying close attention (let the reader understand).

So here is some food for thought. I might not be right, but having an open mind might help us see this major trigger when it does arrive. Antiochus Epiphanes was a proper villain, which

I'll explain in a bit, so we might need to expand our definition of how grand the scale of villainy will be.

Right on the heels of the Sixth Seal, which is the global catastrophe (meteor strike?) that causes widespread death and geographic destruction, the Seventh Seal sneaks in. Nothing happens on Earth, but look at what is described:

> **[Rev 8:1] And when he had opened the seventh seal, there was silence <u>in heaven</u> about the space of half an hour. [2] And I saw the seven angels which stood before God; and to them were given seven trumpets. [3]And another angel came and stood at <u>the altar</u>, having a <u>golden censer</u>; and there was given unto him much <u>incense</u>, that he should <u>offer</u> it with the prayers of all saints upon the golden altar which was before the throne. [4] And the smoke of the incense, which came with the prayers of the saints, ascended up before God out of the angel's hand. [5] And the angel took the censer, and filled it with fire of the altar, and <u>cast it</u> into the earth: and there were voices, and thunderings, and lightnings, and an earthquake.**

Where is this taking place? In Heaven.

What is being described? An altar.

Who is there? An angel that acts like a high priest.

What is it/he doing? Putting incense into a golden censer.

Why is it/he doing this? It's an offering.

How does it end? The offering and mechanism to do another offering is thrown to earth.

Do you see it? This is the REAL Daily Sacrifice! The Seventh Seal is one of the triggers! Right after the Great Day of Tribulation, the Antichrist shows up (start the clock?) on Earth while up in Heaven, the Daily Sacrifice ends. That's when Daniel's clock can really start. Daily Sacrifice on Earth has been stopped by

Satan and Company many times. Yet in this Temple "in Heaven" this mysterious "High Priest" angel continues to make an offering. At the end of the routine, he tosses the golden censer to earth, which means that for the next 1,290, there will be no sacrifices made in heaven. That's what Daniel is talking about.

I'd even offer speculation about this mysterious priest: Melchizedek!

Don't let poor interpretations of Genesis 14 fool you. Melchizedek was not some local dude. He was Heaven's high priest who came down to bless and sanctify Abraham with the Holy Eucharist. Priestly stuff. Abraham seemed to understand and offered tithes. Not buying it? You don't want Melchizedek to be this significant?

Well, check out:

[Hebrews 7:1] For this Melchizedek, king of Salem, priest of the most high God, who met Abraham returning from the slaughter of the kings, and blessed him; [2] To whom also Abraham gave a tenth part of all; first being by interpretation King of righteousness, and after that also King of Salem, which is, King of peace; [3] Without father, without mother, without descent, having neither beginning of days, nor end of life; but made like unto the Son of God; abideth a priest continually.

Priest of the Most High God

(King) of Peace and Righteousness

Divinely made=without father, without mother

Not human=without descent

Immortal=nor end of life

Immortal=no beginning, no end

Divinely made=made like unto the Son of God

Continually=Daily Sacrifice

So my theory is that Melchizedek hangs out in the Temple of Heaven, makes his Daily Sacrifice, pops down to earth on occasion like he did with Abraham (and others? Jacob?), and following the Sixth Seal, this eternal priest stops the Daily Sacrifice and triggers the End Times and the Cosmic Countdown.

The only reason we had all that information dropped about Melchizedek is that Jesus is going to replace this guy as our righteous High Priest. Jesus gave himself as a sacrifice long ago, and once Melchizedek tosses his golden censer to earth, it signals how Jesus will sit on earth with us rather than needing a Heavenly Daily Sacrifice.

How cool is that?

(Or it could be a pig).

An Image of the Beast

If our interpretation of "Daily Sacrifice" is a bit off, then perhaps our interpretation of "Abomination of Desolation" is also a bit off. Again, the historical accounts of Antiochus Epiphanes lean toward the offense being swine related or including a shrine to Zeus. In the grand scheme of things, the pig seems silly and the shrine seems to already be happening with the Temple Mount being a much more extreme version of an old statue.

While the old school definition seems to be a "thing," what if the AofD is a person. Is there support for this theory? Well, both Matthew and Mark's translation use modern English words that become personification when it mentions the AofD "standing" where it should not be." Standing? Standing. So a person—the Antichrist—will stand where it should not be. If it's NOT in a rebuilt temple, then where else could the Antichrist be standing? Why is it an abomination?

The Antichrist stands in Jerusalem, which is a holy place.

The Antichrist (of the 7) stands upon the earth.

My theory is that the Antichrist is a genetic Frankenstein. Like Nebuchadnezzar's nightmare, this figure will be engineered and made up of the seven worst villains in human history. Is there Revelation support for this? Sure is.

The Prophet (we'll get to him later) decides that **"they should make an image to the beast, which had the wound by a sword, and did live."** An image? The simplest way to picture his would be a statue, yet making an "image" of something with genetics is…cloning. In that same Rev 13:14 verse, it establishes that the previous image died. Dead. Killed. While there certainly could be a bit of resurrection, the more impressive feat would be to "clone" someone who's been dead for centuries and bring them back to life. That's science, folks! Clap, clap.

Yet while the DNA lives again, the true measure of scientific immortality would be bringing back the person's soul and re-turning it to the body. If you could rebuild a body and then also bring back consciousness, that'd be super impressive.

> **[Rev 13:15] And he had power to give life unto the image of the beast, that the image of the beast should both speak, and cause that as many as would not worship the image of the beast should be killed.**

Give life? Yep, the Prophet somehow brings back the "speaking" part of a clone. This isn't some statue with a walkie-talkie built in. This act makes people marvel. This act ends the need to fear God. Why? Clone a person and bring their soul back. Done!

So the Abomination of Desolation might simply mean that the Prophet "alakazams" the consciousness "of the 7" into this genetically engineered body. Once the clone breathes life and speaks, the clock starts since it's "**an abomination**."

It's an epic theory, huh?

I'd also like to explore another option that could go along with my clone theory. In 1st Maccabee 1:43, which describes Antiochus Epiphanes. **"Yea, many also of the Israelites consented to his religion, and sacrificed unto idols, and profaned the Sabbath."** I'm not backtracking. AE did the pig/Zeus profaning, but notice that AE had a specific religion. So I did a little reading and the footnotes said "Baal Shamen" was "his religion."

Remember that the term Abomination of Desolation comes from the phrase "Siqquc Shomen," which translates as "Baal of Heaven" or "Baal Shamayim." While "idolatrous worship" is bad and so is anything "that maketh desolation," there seems to be a direct line involving the religions of these Antichrist figures. Nimrod and Semiramis=Baal and Anath. Ramses the Great=Daughter named Anath. Nimrod worships the head. Lamech is likely the head. Alexander restores Nimrod's worship of the Head. Nimrod has roots to Zoroaster. Antiochus Epiphanes's symbolism is Zoroaster.

Round and round it goes.

So let's just speculate that AE's religion was a legitimate thread. What would it cause him to do if it's old enough to go back to Lamech?

Dark Sentences

I saved the best for last. Both Antiochus Epiphane's life and death had a touch of the…supernatural. Quite obviously, he is a lynchpin of prophecy with three different prophecies from Daniel describing the "Abomination of Desolation" as well as the "Daily Sacrifice." While Daniel 12 seems to be specifically given for the End Times and Daniel 11 being so vaguely written that is could be both BC and AD (not sure), the passage found in Daniel 8 also hits on all three concepts yet seems to specifically target the monster born Mithradates.

Why the three passages? Well, I think Antiochus Epiphanes is the "game plan" for the coming Antiochrist (see what I did there).

Both will involve two End Time countdowns.

Both will begin as a "little horn" before claiming power.

Both will persecute the good guys.

Both will blaspheme the God of Heaven.

Both will use false peace to achieve their aims.

Both will mock and/or violate the sanctity of worship.

Both will have connections to a dark religion/figure.

Both will die through divine retribution.

Both will conclude with divine deliverance.

So there is a lot that can be learned by studying this little horn known as Antiochus Epiphanes. While all the above stuff are widely known about AE, there are some very curious phrases that make it seem like this guy was way more of a threat than the silly pig/Zeus incident.

Ponder this: How could a villain destroy the earth? Dr. Evil came up with his "laser" plan. Thanos collected the Infinity

Stones. Henry Ford invented combustion engines to create global warming and melt the earth's polar caps (huh? Darn corporate news). All teasing aside, I think I see a plan devised by Antiochus Epiphanes. Now, not having been around, I'm not really sure how any of it worked, but the text seems to imply he had a very audacious plan: attacking heaven!

Remember, he's not the first to thing/attempt this. Head #2 Nimrod built a tower not just as flood insurance but also to "avenge" himself on God. Had the passive-aggressive language reset button not been hit, he likely would have followed through with his plan. Learning from the mistakes of his predecessors, I think Antiochus Epiphanes dedicated his black heart to the study of the black arts. Unlike Nimrod, who wanted to war against God himself, Antiochus Epiphanes had a very subtle plan. As soon as Daniel put his chapter 12 to paper, the prophecy for the End Times was cemented. Having an understanding mind (see what I did there), Antiochus Epiphanes knew he had to do more than sack the Temple. He knew if he could stop the Daily Sacrifice, he'd start the clock. So what if he abducted or killed the Heavenly High Priest Melchizedek?

Brash, I know. But think of the effect. Just like the clock begins between Seal #6 and Seal #7, if something happened to the High Priest, that clock would start early—before Christ's redemption of humanity—causing the world to end without salvation. That…is a diabolical plan.

So with that concept in mind, I'm going to drop the passage again with (my interpretations) inserted to show you a possible translation.

[Daniel 8:9] And out of one of them came forth a little horn (Antiochus Epiphanes), **which waxed exceedingly great, toward the south** (Egypt), **and toward the east** (Parthia), **and toward the pleasant land** (Israel). **[10] And it waxed great, even to the host of heaven** (angels and company); **and it cast down some of the host and of the stars to the ground** (holy cow, did AE defeat angels), **and stamped upon them** (how did he defeat them?). **[11] Yea, he magnified himself even to the prince of the host** (who? Michael? Satan? Pre-incarnate Jesus?), **and by him the daily sacrifice was taken away** (but not ended! Transferred? Hidden? Taken from Jerusalem to Heaven?), **and the place of his sanctuary was cast down** (the Jerusalem temple?). **[12] And a host was given him against the daily sacrifice by reason of transgression** (dark allies? Fallen angels? Demons?), **and it cast down the truth to the ground; and it practiced, and prospered** (so AE was winning). **[13] Then I heard one saint speaking, and another saint said unto that certain saint which spake, How long shall be the vision concerning the daily sacrifice, and the transgression of desolation, to give both the sanctuary and the host to be trodden under foot?** (some of the prophets/angels were getting nervous) **[14] And he said unto me, Unto two thousand and three hundred days; then shall the sanctuary be cleansed** (literally the Maccabean war prophecy).

(wow)

A bit later, Gabriel adds a bit more to the prophecy with some explanation.

[8:23] And in the latter time of their kingdom, when the transgressors are come to the full, a king of fierce countenance, and understanding dark sentences, shall stand up. (Dark sentences=black magic. How does AE wage war against Heaven?)

[8:24] And his power shall be mighty, but not by his own power: and he shall destroy wonderfully, and shall prosper,

and practice, and shall destroy the mighty (gibbor?) **and the holy people.** (Historically, AE was minor. Spiritually, he might've been the greatest threat. No Jews=No Jesus. No Prophecy=No Salvation).

[8:25] And through his policy also he shall cause craft to prosper in his hand; and he shall magnify himself in his heart, and by peace shall destroy many: he shall also stand up against the Prince of princes; but he shall be broken without hand. (Prince of Princes? Prince of the Host?)

Let's dive into that last phrase. The Prince of Princes could mean a few different things. Remember, Melchizedek is introduced with the title "Prince of Peace" and "Prince of Righteousness" so he is a candidate to be either this Prince of Princes or even the Prince of the Host. Or none of the above.

Obviously, Jesus is the other idea that popped into my head. This would mean a literal war on Heaven since Jesus exists but hasn't come down to earth in bodily form yet.

The third option is that this is referencing Michael the Archangel. Again, AE wages war but fails. With his dark allies, AE makes this last for numerous years. While he is trying to wipe out the Jews on Earth, he is also attacking the Host of Heaven and preventing them from answering the prayers of the oppressed Jews. There is a bit of support for this: Dan 10:13 gives us this scene:

> **[Dan 10:13]But the prince of the kingdom of Persia withstood me one and twenty days: but, lo, Michael, one of the chief princes, came to help me; and I remained there with the kings of Persia.**

Huh? So apparently angels are active in the current events of mankind, and in this case, Michael had to go help another one of his angel buddies who was having a tough time of it. Antiochus targets angels?

The fourth option is a bit more audacious: Satan. Look at how Paul describes Satan in his letter to the Ephesians:

[Eph 2:2] Wherein in time past ye walked according to the course of this world, according to the prince of the power of the air, the spirit that now worketh in the children of disobedience.

Now there is a ton of implied language about Satan having been an angel who also waged war against the Host of Heaven and fell to earth. For example: Is 14:12:

[Is 14:12] How you have fallen from heaven, O star of the morning, son of the dawn! You have been cut down to the earth, You who have weakened the nations! [13] But you said in your heart, I will ascend to heaven; I will raise my throne above the stars of God

My point? As Jesus pointed out in his House Divided sermon, Team Satan and Team Beelzebub might not be on the same page. Leave it to the Sons of Perdition to try to bring about Death and Destruction. Satan? Well, he likely wants to prolong his own life for as long as he can. Satan might want to delay his punishment but unlike Antiochus Epiphanes, he doesn't want the world to end. It's just a theory.

This War in Heaven concept is not just my wild imagination. Jesus makes a very, very strange reference to it.

[Matt 11:12] And from the days of John the Baptist until now the kingdom of heaven suffereth violence, and the violent take it by force. [13] For all the prophets and the law prophesied

until John. [14] And if ye will receive it, this is Elijah, which was for to come. [15] He that hath ears to hear, let him hear.

There Jesus goes again in verse 15. "This is a hard one to understand" LOL.

At first, it seems as if Jesus is saying "From now until now, the kingdom of heaven suffers violence." After all, John the Baptist was a peer. That's a very, very small window for a war in heaven. Oh. Oh. Wait. In verse 14, Jesus changes the equation. He throws out some algebra when he says "this is Elijah," which translates as John the Baptist=Elijah. Remember that Elijah lived around 900 BC. John lived in -.5 BC. If John=John, then that's a pretty short and insignificant war. If John=Elijah, then Jesus is saying the Kingdom of Heaven has suffered much violence over the past several centuries.

That, folks, matches up with the Antiochus Epiphanes theory. Dark sentences, indeed.

So there you have it. That's my speculation on the Seven Heads.

[Rev 17:9] And here is the mind which hath wisdom. The seven heads are seven mountains, on which the woman sitteth. [10] And there are seven kings: five are fallen, and one is, and the other is not yet come; and when he cometh, he must continue a short space. [11] And the beast that was, and is not, even he is the eighth, and is of the seven, and goeth into perdition.

The five that have fallen?

#1 Lamech

#2 Nimrod

#3 Ramses the Great

#4 Alexander the Great (The Lion)

#5 Antiochus Epiphanes (The Bear)

And the "one is" king?

Who was alive when John received the prophecy?

Who's the Leopard?

Let's meet Emperor Domitian!

CHAPTER NINE

DEATH LEOPARD

The current Google factoid claims that there have been 109 Billion humans who've lived upon planet Earth, and if I shrugged and went along with that data, you've just met my five favorite choices for the "many antichrists" that have opposed God and then died. I had to speculate on all five. But head #6? Instead of billions and billions of choices, I had a relatively low number to choose from.

I had to find one who "is."

Easy, right? John knew the dude was alive at the time he received the Apocalypse that became known as the Book of Revelation. Simple.

Well, not even the date is an obvious fact.

You see, there are many mindsets about the literal and figurative meaning of the Book of Revelation even within Christianity. Denominations vary on how to see the only book in the Bible that earns the reader a blessing for reading it.

Some believed in a quick return of Christ. Peter and Paul preached like Jesus was coming back any day. For those first few decades, it was a frenzied sprint. Yet the qualifier used by Jesus was that the Gospel must first be spread to ALL nations. That took much longer than Peter and Paul expected. The concept of Christ's return suddenly became muddy.

Some believed in a long return. Back in the first century, Barnabas put out a theory that the Old Testament mattered because of all the Christ and End Times prophecies within it (agreed). One of his points to the early Christians was that the days of creation had meaning. He reckoned that since a "day is like a thousand years to the Lord" that six days means approximately 6,000 years between Adam and the End Times (I'm not claiming Earth age). In Barnabas's theory, the Millennial Kingdom of 1,000 years is the same as God having the 7th Day as a Sabbath. It is the day of rest. It is a day of worship. At the end of the 7th day…judgment day. So the Barnabas theory is that it'd be another 2,000 years until we get to the Battle of Armageddon. (what? That's now!)

Some believed that all the happily ever after described with New Jerusalem means that we're already living in Paradise since our souls have been saved and it's up to us to fix the world. With this take, the Apostasy of the Church is ignored and we're evolving into a better and better world.

Some believed all the prophecies were simply previewing the destruction of Jerusalem in 70 AD. We're living in the vague millennial kingdom, I guess. Again, my autistic brain might not be as sharp as others, but if a few aspects don't work, it short circuits. This one does not compute for me.

Like I said, it's easy to make claims, so even trying to get a fact like WHEN WAS THE BOOK OF REVELATION WRITTEN can get several answers.

Burning the Nero Theory

There are basically two camps. Camp A includes the preterists, who believe that all the prophecies in Revelation describe events that already took place. They're not fans of any of this speculation. So they believe that it described the destruction of Jerusalem, and thus, the villain had to be around before 70 AD. To them, the only candidate was Nero. Because of this, the Nero theory has spilled into Camp B discussion. Camp B folks are much more literal in their belief in the prophecy.

So who's Nero?

Nero is the 6th Roman Emperor who ruled from 54 to 68 AD, which is getting pretty close to the year Jerusalem was destroyed. He was an entitled rich kid with mother issues. He was a bit effeminate and liked the Greek style compared to the warrior Roman style and as a result, he forbade the killing of gladiators. He didn't even like capital punishment. He was a performer and singer who wanted to please and be popular. This guy was *not* terrifying compared to other Caesars, other world leaders, or our other antichrists.

So why would John be afraid to write this dude's name?

To a preterist, Revelation is about current events. So the whole 666/DCLXVI coded name mark of the beast insinuated that John was afraid to write the name of the world's greatest villain? Plus, Nero was dead two years before Jerusalem burned, and he had nothing to do with it. This whole theory makes my head hurt. Why would there be seven churches in Asia when Christianity hasn't fled the Holy Land yet?

Yes, Nero was a piece of garbage. He's famous for being an entitled diva. He wanted to build a new palace. Folks denied him. So he throws a tantrum. He "fiddled while Rome burned" in legend when he had agents start a fire to burn down enough land for his building project, and then he blamed Christian terrorists for it. Well, this shell game ended up causing enough uproar that both Peter and Paul ended up taking the fall in Nero's land grab. Wicked deeds, but nothing on par with these other guys.

When the political tides turned on this spoiled brat, he ended up killing himself when Romans turned on him. Rome broke out into civil war. A year later, we had new administrators.

Yet for some reason, folks are hung up on Nero. First of all, ask yourself what language John would have used to write Revelations? (In writing to the Turks, did he use Hebrew, Greek, Roman, or Turkish?) Or…what language did he READ when he saw the name 666 on the forehead? Ah, that's another big problem. What numbering system did he see? Yet the Pretersts believe that John used Gematria, a system used by Kabbalists, to secretly encode the name of Nero. With this mindset, he took the Hebrew word for Nero. No, wait. That doesn't work. With this mindset, he took the Hebrew word for NeronKaisar, dropped a bunch of letters to turn it into NronQSR, and then use the Gematria system (why?), and cranked out a numerical code 666 (or is that DCLXVI in Roman numerals). Even in isolation this makes my head hurt, but when you try to make all the other stuff fit the time period, it JUST DOESN'T.

Is 95 "is"?

I've already written **Examining the Beloved Disciple**, which gives an account of John's life, so I'll keep this section brief. Eusebius was a Christian historian (with flaws) who wrote an overview of the first three centuries of Christendom, including the early days. Tradition is that John lived in Ephesus prior to Patmos and also afterwards. One of the traditions has him bringing the Virgin Mary with him to Ephesus.

In his book, Eusebius quotes and cites his way through the years after Christ, which is where much of our traditional knowledge of this period comes from. He tells us that Peter was crucified, how Paul was executed, and several other important deaths. Lots of history. Eusebius confirms that John was a prisoner of Domitian while at Patmos until Nerva succeeded to the throne. How does Eusebius know it was Domitian?

Historians.

Here's a summary of why I trust the 95 AD date (other than logic).

Tertullian, in his **Apology**, speaks of Domitian as having banished some Christians, and afterwards giving them leave to return home: probably intending St. John, and some others.

Origen, explaining something in **Matthew**, says: 'James, the brother of John, was killed with a sword by Herod. And a Roman emperor, as tradition teaches, banished John into the island Patmos for the testimony which he bore to the word of truth.

Victorinus, bishop of Pettaw about 290, again and again says that John was banished by Domitian, and in his reign saw the Revelation.

Jerome, in his *Book of Illustrious Men*, says : "Domitian in the fourteenth year of his reign raising the second persecution after Nero, John was banished into the island Patmos, where he wrote the Revelation."

Sulpicius Severus says that 'John the apostle and evangelist, was banished by Domitian into the island Patmos where he had visions, and where he wrote the book of the Revelation.'

Isidore, of Seville, near the end of the sixth century, says, "Domitian raised a persecution against the Christians. In his time the apostle John having been banished into the island Patmos saw the Revelation."

So like Eusebius, it wasn't a controversial take to bring up the name Domitian. Except for the Preterists, most Biblical Scholars feel pretty confident in putting down the date of 95 AD.

The Boiling Oil Incident

In the spirit of getting off point, I'm going to talk about a famous "tale" involving both John and Domitian. Eusebius also put this story into his big research paper. In the account, Domitian is doing his best to wipe out Christianity by targeting leaders and anyone with "royal blood." Apparently, his bounty hunters were effective and brought him all sorts of victims, who would be tortured in public spectacles for Domitian's approval (remember Nero banned this sort of stuff). One day, they brought Domitian a big fish, well, an old fish. They found this guy in Ephesus, and from his age, they believed he might've been a first generation Christian and a high-ranking member of this terrorist group.

Since this was a special occasion for Emperor Domitian, he wanted it done right. So he had a big vat of oil brought in so that they could boil this fellow alive. Domitian and friends gathered, the prisoner was brought in, and the signal was given. But when this old geezer was lowered into the vat of boiling oil—NOTHING HAPPENED! Apparently, when Christ says "If I will that he tarry till I come, what is that to thee?" it's how rumors of immortality get started (John 21:22). Well, the oil obeyed Jesus and refused to harm John, which is about when evil Domitian began to realize that the old man in front of him once said, **"Lord, do You want us to command fire to come down from heaven and consume them?"** (Luke 9:54) That guy was getting annoyed in lukewarm oil.

Freaked out, Domitian changes plans. He's suddenly afraid of this guy and being an inversed believer in God (God is the bad guy to him), he believes John could destroy him and all of Rome. So if you can't kill him?

Domitian sends him to a remote island.

Clever idea.

Why?

You see, Patmos is not a penal colony filled with thousands of hardened criminals. Domitian likely knows how "heroes of the faith" can evangelize, so John is sent to one of the Mediterranean's most remote and barren islands. Putting him there means he can't evangelize anybody. Even if the rumors of immortality are true, this old guy can just twiddle his thumbs for another 2,000 years.

When Domitian dies in 95 AD, John is released from his island prison. As Eusebius writes: **"At that time too the**

apostle John, after his exile on the island, resumed his residence at Ephesus, as the early Christian tradition records."

So…that's why I'm sticking with IS=95 AD.

A Leopard Can't Change His Spots

Unfortunately, there is hardly ANY Biblical ammunition for analyzing Domitian. Antiochus and Alexander got entire chapters of Daniel. Ramses the Great fills the opening pages of Exodus. Even Lamech gets a paragraph of text. But Domitian? Everything we know about him is from the historical records, and considering how much his predecessors HATED him, I'm not sure they paid the biographers very much.

Yet if you do go back to Daniel, he included his dream of the four beasts, who in my estimation, were the remaining 4 kings still to come.

The Lion…Alexander the Great.

The Bear…Antiochus Epiphanes

The next one?

[Daniel 7:6] After this I beheld, and lo another, like a leopard, which had upon the back of it four wings of a fowl; the beast had also four heads; and dominion was given to it.

That's all folks.

It's not super obvious, and folks could twist and turn the meanings to fit anybody.

Like this…

Domitian has 8 letters and Dominion has 8 letters and 6 of 8 match! Gasp! (sorry, I'm still teasing the Nero camp).

Is there symbolism with a leopard?

Um, sure, they ate people in nature. So leopards are obviously a symbol for power and strength. Despite just being a big cat, they're also symbolically brave and bold, full of confidence. Oh, and they also represent a kind of shape shifting, which is gnarly. There are several leopard lines in the Old Testament, but they all seem to be literal big cats. Yet I'd like to remind you about our visual clues about the Antichrist:

> **[Rev 13:2] And the beast which I saw was like unto a leopard, and his feet were as the feet of a bear, and his mouth as the mouth of a lion: and the dragon gave him his power, and his seat, and great authority.**

Stuff like this is why I put so much stock in Daniel's prophecies. Lion, bear, Leopard, oh my!

A History of Violence

The biggest problem I had with researching Domitian is that there was a ton of information on him. So much information, in fact, that when I gleaned information, it became shockingly easy to build a super villain. So I'll admit that "cherry-picking" factoids about Domitian isn't a super strong argument, especially since I began with generic history. Remember, I'm not trying to write for the history books in an unbiased method. I'm biased. And this dude frightens me.

Domitian was born in 51 AD during the reign of Claudius. He was three when Nero became Emperor, 13 when Rome burned, and a tender youth of 17 when Nero took his own life. Unlike Nero, he didn't grow up believing he'd rule. His father, Vespasian, was a general known for his invasion of Britain in 43

AD and served Nero out in the empire. Domitian has an older brother (born 39 AD) who also became a famous general while serving in Germania. They were an ambitious family trying to play the political game. From what I can tell, Vespasian and Titus were away while Domitian and his mother stayed in Rome.

Then the pieces on the chessboard began to move.

Nero is often described as effeminate. Domitian is (later) often described as homophobic. So about the time Domitian is hitting maturity, war breaks out in Judea in 66 AD. Domitian's dad and brother both get "fired" and then reassigned to the hot mess in Judea. It's like they were getting punished for something. Plus, this was Nero's way of keeping them away from Rome.

Something's fishy.

Things in Judea were strange. After surrounding Jerusalem, the Roman commander withdrew and got massacred shortly after. So in 67 AD, Vespasian and Titus showed up with 60,000 soldiers to deal with the emboldened Jews. As dad was systematically taming Judea, things got crazy in Rome. It seems someone was stoking unrest against Nero. Hmm? So Nero kills himself in 68 AD.

It became "The Year of the Four Emperors."

Galba took Caesarship from Spain (Emperor #1). While "someone" stoked internal revolt in Rome, Vitellius (Emperor #3) stokes external revolt. Back in Judea, Vespasian throws his hat in with the rebels and prepares to return, leaving Titus in charge of Judea.

Got it?

Another guy named Otho (Emperor #2) gets in the game, bribes the Praetorian Guard to kill Galba, and then kills himself when he loses a battle to Vitellius. That was quick.

So here comes Vitellius (Emperor #3) to march on Rome, where Domitian lives who tries to get Vitellius to abdicate (bold proposal, huh?). Even though Vitellius *tries* to kill young Domitian (I wonder why?), it fails. Domitian has an ally, Primus. Thanks to his dad and brother, the military is fully rebelling, and Primus leads the Danubian legions to retake Rome. Primus ends up killing Vitellius.

And then something very, very strange happens.

He names Domitian the Emperor.

At 18.

Ha, ha, ha, LOL, says another general named Mucianus, who quickly explains to Primus that the military coup is supporting the *dad* not the youngest son. Nevermind.

And Vespasian becomes Emperor #4.

Dad Needs to Die

Vespasian ends the Julio-Claudio Dynasty as "the help" ends up ruling the Empire just like Horemheb ended the Egyptian Dynasty. Oh, hey, that's a trait! There's probably a good reason why paranoid Nero sent him to Judea in 67 since he ends up on the throne less than two years after this insult. From there, Vespasian rules Rome for the next decade and brings stability to the empire. It's all a bit boring.

Unless you're Jewish.

Oh, yes, there was major conflict still happening in Jerusalem, and once the civil war ends in Rome, Vespasian unleashes

Titus to annihilate the Jews, which he does. According to historian Josephus, it's about as bad as it gets. Seriously, it's a disgusting, disturbing event that leaves the Temple in rubble. The priestly "daily sacrifice" was certainly ended. Yet Vespasian isn't done. He begins a genocidal policy by hunting down any Jew from the royal line of David. With the Jewish thorn removed from his side, he celebrates and promotes Titus with the Arch of Titus.

And Domitian?

Nothing. Dad purposefully prevents Domitian from attaining any position of power during those ten years. So about the time Domitian is 28, his dad suddenly comes down with a case of deadly diarrhea and dies. Poison?

Titus only sits on the throne for two years. Like his father and other emperors, he declares himself to be a god. Although a fair ruler, he had some very bad luck (Mount Vesuvius blew up) and had barely gotten himself comfortable when he also died from poisoning. This time, folks realized it might be more than just unlucky diarrhea. The historian Philostratus even had a suspect and method: Domitian with a sea hare in the farmhouse. Solving the game of clue didn't really matter. Domitian had become emperor.

Twelve years after having had the crown taken away, Domitian becomes emperor of Rome and rules for fifteen years, and by many accounts, was considered to be one of Rome's most efficient administrators ever. He overhauled the military and helped it achieve its peak efficiency. Not bad for being Antichrist Head #5.

Oh, that's right. John said somebody alive was the 5th head of the Antichrist.

The Dark Deeds of Domitian

This guy freaked out the Romans. Despite not being in the military, he strutted around in a general's uniform and displayed an unhealthy interest in warfare. He also implemented horrifying penalties for crimes that went far beyond law and order. His homophobia took barbaric turns when he mercilessly killed his lead general Saturninus, displayed his head as a trophy, and then tried to erase him from history. Nero PTSD? Being a bad guy does not qualify you as one of the great villains in history. Is there more?

Yes, Domitian declares himself as a deity, but what Roman didn't? Yes, he upgrades it so that he is the sole deity to be worshiped, but hey, that's a big ego. Yet it is private actions that were so intriguing. Apparently, he brought back some of Rome's ancient religions. Roman mythology had been whitewashed during the Alexander era and thus it's hard to distinguish where Greek mythology ends and Roman mythology begins. So Domitian dedicates his power to uncovering the ancient rites. Sound familiar?

Just like Ramses the Great disregarded traditional Egyptian mythology to worship a dead god (Seth) and a virgin warrior goddess (Anath), Domitian digs up and worships a four-headed Minerva. Who's Minerva? Heck, even ten-year-old Jason Willis knows that one. Minerva is the Roman name for Athena, a virgin warrior goddess…

Oh.

Since Minerva normally doesn't have four-heads, it's unclear what the heck Domitian is worshiping here. The goddess of witchcraft, Hecate (see MacBeth), is a three-headed goddess. Does that count? Perhaps. Hecate is pretty old. The four faces of Minera?

Here's my theory:

Semiramis (Nimrod)

Anath (Ramses)

Athena (Alexander)

Minerva (Antiochus)

The virgin-warrior goddess theme seems to be a common thread, and considering Semiramis crowned herself as the "Queen of Heaven," it wouldn't shock me if Domitian's quest to uncover the past led him to his Sons of Perdition conclusion. One of the historians I read described how Domitian would invite powerful Romans to his private dinner parties and they'd be so "black and funeral" that his guests would be "paralyzed with fear." How's that for dark?

Don't forget that there is limited Biblical text about this "beast" but what else did the leopard have in its description?

[Daniel 7:6] After this I beheld, and lo another, like a leopard, which had upon the back of it four wings of a fowl; the beast had also four heads; and dominion was given to it.

Yep, there's the four heads. Still not sure what this means, but it's enough for me.

Aside from all of that creepy stuff, he continues the policy of hunting down the royal bloodline. Why would you do that? Think about it. Judea has been ruled by non-Jews for centuries now. They're not hunting down Herod's Idomenean bloodline.

They're hunting down the Davidic line. Why would a Roman care? Domitian is not an atheist. Like Nimrod and Antiochus Epiphanes, he likely believes in a Creator but sees God as his enemy. Killing God's favorite people is the closest he can get to God.

Eusebius brings up an anecdote about how his bounty hunters brought him two grandsons of Jude. Who? Well, the bounty hunters had to explain that Joseph and Clopas were brothers, and according to Jewish tradition, when one brother dies, the children...yada, yada, yada...brothers of Jesus! Except instead of Jude, they bring him the grandchildren of Jude. In the only merciful moments involving Domitian, he is disgusted by these gruff, calloused men and felt they were too pathetic to be worthy of kingship and refused to follow through with the planned execution. The two grandsons outlived Domitian and became early church leaders.

Near the end of his rule, John is brought to him and (oil anecdote here), John ends up exiled on Patmos. Meanwhile, in Rome, Domitian's reign of terror continued to the bitter end. According to Suetonius, Domitian's dark magic gave him a pretty good clue about when he was going to die, including the time of day. So Domitian safeguarded himself as the day and hour approached. But his servants tricked him by lying to him about the time, and when he relaxed his guard, a servant named Stephanus stabbed him in the groin while claiming to have information on the assassination plot. That's funny. In true Domitian fashion, he murders his own assassin before succumbing to his wounds.

Rome hated this guy so much that there were no grand send offs or funerals. Without any children, the senators picked a new emperor. Upon taking the throne, Nerva passed a decree, ***damnatio memoriae,*** that required all memories of Domitian to be erased from history. Coins and statues were melted, his arches were torn down, and his name was erased from all public records.

And John went home to Ephesus and started writing letters to the Christian Churches in Asia. Ding, dong, Domitian's dead, but the scariest king was still to come.

CHAPTER TEN

AN EVIL THOUGHT

The Beloved Disciple is freed from his exile on the island of Patmos and is allowed to return home to Ephesus. From the clues found in the Book of Revelation, it appears as if he actively writes the visions as he is shown the future. Heck, there's even times he's told to "not write" some of the visions. When the day comes to be released, the 5+1+1=7=8 prophecy has already been changed to 6+1=7=8 since Domitian just got killed. Since John was there on the Mount of Olives and on Patmos, he's beginning to understand that the **"gospels must first be preached to all nations"** clause in the prophecy means that Christianity has a long road ahead of it before the Beast/Antichrist prophecy happens.

And the clue? Thanks to the obvious Seal 6 prophecy (and sneaky Seal 7 right after it), the arrival of the Antichrist to power will be marked with one of the most devastating fireworks shows humanity has ever seen. Vesuvius? Please. Tsunamis? Are you kidding? The disaster described in Seal 6 and elsewhere in the

Bible will be so obvious and unmistakable that not a single historian will miss it.

Which means since the Year 95 AD, we haven't seen anything even close. Nada. Nothing. There hasn't been anything on record where the whole planet goes kaput in a single day. Plus, the Antichrist is only going to be given 3 ½ years before Jesus returns and brings Armageddon with him. That hasn't happened. Jesus hasn't returned.

So what's the deal with the delay?

Daniel Chapter 2 contains Nebuchadnezzar's "nightmare" about the worst of these eight figures, who is made up of parts. Again, I like to see this prophecy as both an Antichrist prophecy and also a "passage of time." Daniel and Nebuchadnezzar were shown the progression of empires that would lead to the End Times.

Head of Gold=Babylon

Silver=Persia

Brass=Greece

So far, so good. Well, who conquered the Greek empire? That was Rome. So that seems to indicate that Iron=Rome. Our next ingredient was the "Miry Clay" which doesn't seem to help at all. Following the collapse of the Roman Empire, who stepped up to the plate? Genghis Khan? Napoleon? The clarity of this era certainly is miry.

> **[Daniel 2:45] Forasmuch as thou sawest that the stone was cut out of the mountain without hands, and that it brake in pieces the iron, the brass, the clay, the silver, and the gold; the great God hath made known to the king <u>what shall come to pass</u> hereafter: and the dream is certain, and the interpretation thereof sure.**

So aside from the big "Frankenstein" metaphor, the other clue is that the prophecy is trying to show the passage of time. It seems that following four powerful dynasties, the era of the 7th Head is…muddy.

Considering the 10 Horns

Yet Antichrist Head #7 seems to be tied to the End Times. Take a look at the passage again:

> **[Rev 17:10] And there are seven kings: five are fallen, and one is, and the other is not yet come; and when he cometh, he must continue <u>a short space</u>. [11] And the beast that was, and is not, even he is the eighth, and is of the seven, and goeth into perdition. [12] And the ten horns which thou sawest <u>are ten kings</u>, which have received no kingdom as yet; but receive power as kings one hour with the beast. [13] These have one mind, and shall give their power and strength unto the beast.**

So aside from being in John's future, Head #7 is given a clue that "**he must continue a short space.**" There is also the mention of the ten horns. If you focus on that clue for a bit, Daniel gives us a bit more. **"These great beasts, which are four, are four kings, which shall arise out of the earth."** To recap Daniel, he saw in 600ish BC that there were four beasts in his future. My simple recap is:

Lion with plucked wings=Alexander the Great

Bear that devours three ribs=Antiochus Epiphanes

Leopard with four heads and dominion=Domitian

And Iron Man=Robert Downey Jr.

Oh, wait. Perhaps we should look at that verse closely. Notice how the metaphors went from organic and natural to industrial and metallic. Huh? Agrarian society. Industrial society.

[Daniel 7:7] After this I saw in the night visions, and behold a fourth beast, dreadful and terrible, and strong exceedingly; and it had great iron teeth: it devoured and brake in pieces, <u>and stamped the residue</u> with the feet of it: and it was diverse from all the beasts that were before it; <u>and it had ten horns</u>. [8] I considered the horns, and, behold, there came up among them <u>another little horn</u>, before whom there were three of the first horns plucked up by the roots: and, behold, in this horn were eyes like the eyes of man, and a mouth speaking great things.

A fascinating clue found in the description of this beast is that it has 10 horns, and that "secret society" of 10 leaders will transition from the failure of Head #7 and follow up with the "little horn" that will become the Antichrist.

So this is why I feel it's important to connect #7 and #8 together. When I started to make a list, I realized I had 18-19 centuries to look through. Having looked at the previous candidates, I knew there were certain traits described:

Obviously evil!

Knowing but Rejecting God.

Predestined, "Not of Us."

"Son of Perdition" or "Son of Belial" connection.

Changes "law."

Spiritually or Politically powerful.

So while there might've been some powerful Polynesian sorcerer in the 340s, or a psychopathic killer in India in the 780s, or a crazed horse lord that conquered vast areas of real estate, it was pretty easy to overlook entire centuries and continents. Knowing that the "ten horns" connection exists, and that I was born in 1971 and PRIOR to Seal #6 also helped me eliminate candidates. Luckily, I also had another clue to analyze.

Devouring The Whole Earth

After Daniel received his vision of the four beasts, the angel stepped up and did some explaining that went beyond iron. Here's the rest of the insight into the prophecy:

> **[Daniel 7:23] Thus he said, The fourth beast shall be the fourth kingdom upon earth, which shall be diverse from all kingdoms, and shall <u>devour the whole earth</u>, and shall tread it down, and break it in pieces.**

Just like the first seal seems to mandate that the gospel must be preached to ALL NATIONS, which means James, Peter, Andrew, and John better learn how to play the didgeridoo, the fourth beast is also going to create chaos on a GLOBAL scale. There has been plenty of violence. There has been plenty of war. There has been plenty of evil. So how is this iron-toothed kingdom going to be different than Rome or Greece?

Before we answer, let's review these two GLOBAL qualifiers.

In my mental movie, I see Jesus freaking out his four key disciples during his Mount of Olives conversation about the end times. This is what he said to them:

> **[Matt 24:6] And ye shall hear of wars and rumors of wars: see that ye be not troubled: for all these things must come to pass, but the end is not yet. [7] For nation shall rise against nation, and kingdom against kingdom: and there shall be famines,**

and pestilences, and earthquakes, in diverse places. [8] All these are the beginning of sorrows.

The beginning? Global war will mean "the end is not yet." To get them to calm down, he brings up the fact that the gospel must first be preached to all nations BEFORE any of this stuff happens. To me, that is Seal #1—the White Horse. Wrapping a scroll in seals means that the message can't be read until ALL the seals are uncracked, usually in order. Seal #1=Preaching

The second seal also seems to fit the other global qualifier we have. Antichrist Head #7 will do something nobody has done before. So let's review the second seal:

[Rev 6:3] And when he had opened the second seal, I heard the second beast say, Come and see. [4]And there went out another horse that was red: and power was given to him that sat thereon to take peace <u>from the earth</u>, and that they should kill one another: and there was given unto him a great sword.

While not quite as specific as the other prophecy about war, this one also explains that before we get to the Antichrist showing up, we're going to have war on the whole earth. Napoleon never got to Australia or America, did he? Before him, crazy kings had to walk their troops from nation to nation. So when you look at the death toll of wars during the last two thousand years (yes, I went there), the stats are pretty obvious. The best the Romans could muster? Three million in a regional war. Elsewhere, China puts this body count to shame with 36 million during the An Lushan Rebellion, but the problem with this frontrunner is that it is also quite regional (bet you didn't even know about it). The Mongols ranged between two continents and also rang up a 40 million death toll, but on the other side of the planet? No one took notice.

When you get to World War One, suddenly you've got a runner up. With up to 40 million killed on both sides of the sphere, this is finally a unique war different from the others. But the reason for fighting it? Old school. A few years later, we get World War Two with 80 million, the technically largest war ever fought, but if you toss in the Soviets, Chinese, and Japanese, the impact gets even larger. Why was this war started? (save that thought).

Before I say it aloud, I want to bring up something else about our Antichrists. While they are all very obviously "anti-God," these Sons of Perdition are NOT atheists. They believe. You don't build the Tower of Babel if you don't believe you can stab God. They all have dark religions, don't they? So I'm going to eliminate a bunch of communist leaders for this reason, which leads me back to a leader who dared go beyond the Gates of the Magogoli.

The Armies of Gog and Magog

So before we lift the curtain to reveal that sinister mustache, there was another unique prophecy that spans antiquity to the future—Gog and Magog. Despite it being referenced from Genesis to Revelations, there is hardly any consensus among scholars as to what this term actually means. Yes, we have a descendant of Japheth, which means the culture is likely "European" but many tribes moved all over. The Goths (one of the leading Gog theories) started in Scandinavia, moved through Western Europe, and ended up way over by the Black Sea. Celts? Germans? Russians? I've read several theories.

Here's one of my custom theories: supernatural.

I'm not sure if I'm serious, but consider the death toll of the Bowls of Wrath poured out onto the earth following the Sixth Seal. At the end of it, following the Battle of Armageddon, God pummels the earth with hailstones larger than cannonballs. Is there anything living after this? Yet a thousand years afterwards, this is what happens:

> **[Rev 20:7] And when the thousand years are expired, Satan shall be loosed out of his prison, [8] And shall go out to deceive the nations which are in the four quarters of the earth, Gog and Magog, to gather them together to battle: the number of whom is as the sand of the sea.**

Where did they come from? Where did they hide? Caves? Outer Space? A Colony on Mars? Regardless of HOW they escaped the Bowls of Wrath, they come back with Satan to finish what the Antichrist failed to accomplish. That's a determined enemy.

So between Japheth and Satan, there's another significant passage involving Gog and Magog. It's pretty muddy, so I'll drop the whole thing onto the page and then identify the most curious phrases:

> **[Ezekiel 38:1] And the word of the LORD came unto me, saying, [2] Son of man, set thy face against Gog, the land of Magog, the chief prince of Meshech and Tubal, and prophesy against him, [3] And say, Thus saith the Lord GOD; Behold, I am against thee, O Gog, the chief prince of Meshech and Tubal: [4] And I will turn thee back, and put hooks into thy jaws, and I will bring thee forth, and all thine army, horses**

and horsemen, all of them clothed with all sorts of armor, even a great company with bucklers and shields, all of them handling swords: [5] Persia, Ethiopia, and Libya with them; all of them with shield and helmet: [6] Gomer, and all his bands; the house of Togarmah of the north quarters, and all his bands: and many people with thee. [7] Be thou prepared, and prepare for thyself, thou, and all thy company that are assembled unto thee, and be thou a guard unto them. [8] <u>After many days</u> thou shalt be visited: <u>in the latter years</u> thou shalt come into the land that is brought back from the sword, and is gathered out of many people, against the mountains of Israel, which have been always waste: but it is brought forth out of the nations, and they shall dwell safely all of them. [9] Thou shalt ascend and come <u>like a storm</u>, thou shalt be <u>like a cloud</u> to cover the land, thou, and all thy bands, and many people with thee.[10] Thus saith the Lord GOD; It shall also come to pass, that at the same time shall things come into thy mind, and thou shalt think <u>an evil thought</u>: [11] And thou shalt say, I will go up to <u>the land of unwalled villages</u>; I will go to them that are at rest, that dwell safely, all of them <u>dwelling without walls</u>, and having neither bars nor gates, [12] <u>To take a spoil</u>, and to take a prey; to turn thine hand upon the desolate places that are now inhabited, and upon the people that are gathered out of the nations, which have gotten cattle and goods, that dwell in the midst of the land. [13] Sheba, and Dedan, and the merchants of Tarshish, with all the young lions thereof, shall say unto thee, Art thou come to take a spoil? hast thou gathered thy company to take a prey? to carry away silver and gold, to take away cattle and goods, to take a great spoil? [14] Therefore, son of man, prophesy and say unto Gog, Thus saith the Lord GOD; <u>In that day</u> when my people of Israel dwelleth safely, shalt thou not know it? [15] And thou shalt come from thy place out <u>of the north parts</u>, thou, and many people with thee, all of them riding upon horses, <u>a great company, and a mighty army</u>: [16] And thou shalt come up against my people of Israel, as a cloud to cover the land; it shall be <u>in the latter days</u>, and I will bring thee against my land, that the heathen may know me, when I shall be sanctified in thee, O Gog, before their eyes.

[17] Thus saith the Lord GOD; Art thou he of whom I have spoken in old time by my servants the prophets of Israel, which prophesied in those days many years that I would bring thee against them? [18] And it shall come to pass at the same time when <u>Gog shall come against the land of Israel</u>, saith the Lord GOD, that my fury shall come up in my face. [19] For in my jealousy and in the fire of my wrath have I spoken, Surely in that day there shall be a great shaking in the land of Israel; [20] So that the fishes of the sea, and the fowls of the heaven, and the beasts of the field, and all creeping things that creep upon the earth, and all the men that are upon the face of the earth, shall shake at my presence, and the mountains shall be thrown down, and the steep places shall fall, and every wall shall fall to the ground. [21] And I will call for a sword against him throughout all my mountains, saith the Lord GOD: every man's sword shall be against his brother. [22] And I will plead against him with pestilence and with blood; and I will rain upon him, and upon his bands, and upon the many people that are with him, an overflowing rain, and <u>great hailstones, fire, and brimstone.</u> [23] Thus will I magnify myself, and sanctify myself; and I will be known in the eyes of many nations, and they shall know that I am the LORD.

[Ezekiel 39:21] And I will set my glory <u>among the heathen</u>, and all the heathen shall see my judgment that I have executed, and my hand that I have laid upon them. [22] So the house of Israel shall know that I am the LORD their God from that day and forward. [23] And the heathen shall know that <u>the house of</u>

Israel went into captivity for their iniquity: because they trespassed against me, therefore hid I my face from them, and gave them into the hand of their enemies: so fell they all by the sword. [24] According to their uncleanness and according to their transgressions have I done unto them, and hid my face from them.[25] Therefore thus saith the Lord GOD; Now will I bring again the captivity of Jacob, and have mercy upon the whole house of Israel, and will be jealous for my holy name; [26] After that they have borne their shame, and all their trespasses whereby they have trespassed against me, when they dwelt safely in their land, and none made them afraid. [27] When I have brought them again from the people, and gathered them out of their enemies' lands, and am sanctified in them in the sight of many nations; [28] Then shall they know that I am the LORD their God, which caused them to be led into captivity among the heathen: but I have gathered them unto their own land, and have left none of them any more there. [29] Neither will I hide my face any more from them: for I have poured out my spirit upon the house of Israel, saith the Lord GOD.

Ezekiel Unpacked

So one of the unique aspects about this passage is how Ezekiel is told several times that this prophecy isn't right around the corner. This prophecy is about THE LATTER DAYS. We're not talking about Israel 1.0 (Moses to Babylon) or Israel 2.0 (Babylon to Antiochus) or Israel 3.0 (Antiochus to Domitian). Nope, we're talking about an Israel that doesn't live in Israel. For Ezekiel, that was a very, very distant future. This warning was both for Gog and for the Jews. Once again, after Domitian and Rome erased Israel from the map, the Jews left for countries all across Europe. A common Ashkenzi Jew migration showed settlement in France and then a migration into central Europe. Yes, there was heavy persecution throughout that time, but this resilient people soon found themselves living in their enemies' lands rather than the Holy Land.

The iniquity? Well, Israel 1.0 got punished for Solomon's sins and ended up in Babylon. Israel 2.0 turned to the Greek way of living and the Maccabee era dealt with that iniquity. Israel 3.0? Oh, yeah, they rejected Jesus. So this great diaspora from the Holy Land to Europe is God's punishment for that. Yet as we get close to THE LATTER DAYS, God has a unique punishment that'll get the attention of Jews and the Heathen nations.

So in the 1900s, Jewish leaders, who'd become wealthy through international banking, began to imagine a return to the Holy Lands, now filled with poor Palestinians. World War I shook things up, leaving Palestine suddenly up for grabs and Europe a bit unpleasant. But it didn't happen until 1948.

And what happened after World War I?

An evil thought!

Notice how this prophecy establishes Gog and Magog as a "northern" country. This unnamed northern country strikes like a storm (blitzkrieg?) and finds the Jews dwelling without walls. Well, that's exactly what happened in the Holocaust, isn't it? They lived in dozens of European countries, and when Nazi Germany rose to power, they struck quickly. The mighty army of the Germans defeated over a dozen countries and formed alliances with **Persia, Ethiopia, and Libya** (and Italy? Japan?) to form the Axis Powers. War spread to the four corners of Earth. Now, if Nazi Germany had been left uncontested, it would have globally wiped out the Jews and then turned on the other non-Aryan races. That, folks, is <u>an evil thought.</u> It made this war so much different than others.

And who came up with this plan? Obviously, I'm now naming Adolph Hitler as my Head #7, but he isn't the one who came up with the plan.

<u>An Evil Thought</u>

Of all the rabbit holes I've gone down, the darkest, slimiest hole might've been an exploration of what Gnostic means. On the surface, Gnosis means knowledge, which seems like a good thing. Knowledge is power! Yet if Christ is the light, and the Antichrist is darkness, then the same thing goes for God being light and Gnosis being darkness. The Gnostics do not deny a Creator or religion but instead flip it all around in a Bizarro World. In a nutshell, the Creator is evil, Satan is a champion of justice, and the very thing God created and declared good—flesh and the material world—is bad. I could keep going and going. The history and its slippery opposition to Christianity goes back centuries and centuries. John dealt with Gnostics in his elder years. Peter dealt with a Gnostic named Simon the Magus. Yet Gnosticism isn't just a flawed version of Christianity meant to confuse early Christians about Gospel names, it seems to go back centuries and centuries BC. It might be the religion of Perdition and the Darkness.

What about Hitler?

If little old me can find the Gnostic Rabbit Hole so easily, it's no wonder others in the modern world have also found it. We'll return to the Gnostic Rabbit Hole for Chapter 12, but just trust me that unlike Vikings rowing into Europe to kill Christians, Gnostics have a very organized agenda. They are the Anti. (I have so much more I want to say. Sigh…)

Well, in going down this Gnostic Rabbit hole, I ran right into Hitler's mentors. We'll get to Eckhart and Blavatsky in a bit. I'll admit that there is a ton of fan-fiction when it comes to Hitler, so you could stop reading this chapter and think: Hitler…Holocaust…Head #7. What else do you need for evidence?

Long ago, I came across this saying from an Anishinaabe elder: What the People Believe is True. Jimbob writes a book. Pedro writes a book. The book that sells the most is the fact. So when I'm reading about history or the Bible, I don't put much stock into either Jimbob or Pedro since history is so speculative. My point? I read a bunch of World War II books for this next section.

Hitler's His-Story

We'll start with Adolph's family tree. The forty-year-old Catholic virgin, Maria Anna Schicklgruber has inherited plenty of money but has no love. She has a chance encounter with a mysterious Jewish man named Leopold Frankenberger. This Catholic-Jewish tryst results in Alois Schicklgruber being born, who then changes his name to Hitler. Alois Hitler married Klara Polzl and they produced young Adolf on April 20, 1889.

The name Hitler has roots in the following meanings: shepherd, hut, guard.

Young Adolf followed a simple Cistercian lifestyle of farming and beekeeping, developed a fixation on warfare, fought frequently with his father, thought about joining the church, and then became a total punk.

By 16, he left home to live the bohemian life in Vienna, where he learned to hate both Jews and Catholics, apparently. By 20, he was living in a homeless shelter, and by 24, he was living in Munich.

World War I took him away from his poverty. He was decorated for bravery for his time as a dispatch runner. While the war gave him glory, it also took away his...um...well, he got wounded in the groin. By 1919, he became an intelligence officer and infiltrated the German Workers Party, and within four years, he is arrested for high treason and goes to prison where he writes about his struggle.

Oh, and he met Dietrich Eckart.

This is where the story of Hitler takes a sharp right turn.

The Thule Society

If Hitler is Batman then Dietrich Eckart is Robin. Better put, if Hitler is an Antichrist then Eckart is his prophet. Eckart was a Bavarian Catholic who had a dark turn into the occult. He dove into Aleister Crowley, Nostradamus, John Dee, Richard Wagner, and even Mozart as he developed an idea for a "New World Order" which manifested as a Third Reich.

That guy.

Thanks to the bright light cast by historians, even this super-secret stuff came to the surface following the Holocaust. Eckart (1868-1923) was doing all the heavy lifting long before Hitler showed up.

Although he didn't invent the Thule Society, Eckart handed off all these dark philosophies to Hitler. For the Thule Society, they believed there once was a place called Hyperborea, a white island refuge of superbeings. Like Atlantis or the Tower of Babel, this society was destroyed by a disaster and its survivors dispersed across the earth. Spiritually, they believed if they could reconnect to this old society, they would awaken "universal energy field" that would "awaken the sleeping powers within." Fun!

The upper echelon of this secret society became known as the Brotherhood of Death, and they took it upon themselves to find what was lost. The Ahnenerbe became this pseudo-scientific research group that began researching the heritage of the survivors, now known as the Aryans. Himmler would later help bring this plan to fruition, but long before that, Eckart was the one putting this plan together.

Since the Thule survivors were almost godlike, the Thule Society believed they could use genetics (Thanks for the idea, Henry Ford), to locate and bring back these superior genes while also eliminating the inferior genes, the Jewish people. Apparently, the Jews were the spiritual enemies of the old Aryans (sounds like Nimrod vs. Abram). Their research led them to use symbols connected to "Brahmins, Masons, Rosicrucians, and Templars." They believed if they could find their prophet and arm him properly, he'd bring back this old society. The innermost circle was privy to the "hard core gnostic teachings on the grail."

Gnostic?

H.P. Blavatsky

(told ya Gnosticism was an issue). Helena was born in 1831, a century before Hitler would begin the Holocaust. Heck, she's not even German. This entitled, aristocratic Ukrainian developed an obsession with the occult and history of the Carolingians, Germanic Knights, and the Crusades. For the time period, she was given a modern education yet still found herself given in marriage to a wealthy man named Blavatsky. Her wealth lets her continue to explore her occult interests and she becomes a world traveler that visits dozens and dozens of foreign countries. During a trip to London, she meets "the Teacher" who brings her focus to the study of secret knowledge in a secret place. Do you remember where Alexander wanted to go? Yep, she goes to the "master in Tibet" for pseudo-historical studies.

At 40, Helena dusts off ancient gnosticism and packages it as new. So what?

Well, here is where it begins to manifest a result.

"Adolph Hitler read Madame Blavatsky's book, *The Secret Doctrine,* nightly. That was the source of his power and ability to control others. After the war, Winston Churchill suppressed efforts to expose Hitler's occultism."

And what's so bad about *The Secret Doctrine?*

"One of the most hidden secrets involves the so-called fall of angels. Satan and his rebellious host will thus prove to have become direct saviors and creators of divine man. Thus Satan, once he ceases to be viewed in the superstitious spirit of the church, grows into the grandiose image."

And check out this:

"It is Satan who is the God of our planet and the only God. Satan (or Lucifer) represents the centrifugal energy of the Universe, this ever-living symbol of self-sacrifice for the intellectual independence of humanity."

Hitler never meets Helena, but through Dietrich Eckhart, this **Secret Doctrine** described by Blavatsky fuels the Thule Society and Nazism.

The Long Awaited Messiah

So Eckhart searched for clues about Hyperborea and for the messiah who'd help them restore the earth. He and the Thule Society believed Hitler was their man. Apparently, Hitler believed he was the man also. At 15, Hitler listened to Richard Wagner's Master Race and found himself spiritually possessed during the songs. This made him seek out the Thule Society. Once he connected with them, Hitler had "unknown superiors" who then taught Hitler. These masters became Hitler's "guiding voice of providence" and according to Hermann Rauschning, even the military powers were "oblivious to the powers controlling them."

Do I believe all this? There's stuff on the Protocols of the Learned Elders of Zion, the Bilderberg Group, the Dragon Court, the Trilateral Commission the Knights of Malta, and the European Council of Princes (33 royal houses who claimed descent from Jesus. Ew!). This is the swampy bottom of the rabbit hole, folks.

What did Hitler do to make me think there might be real connections?

First of all, he went where Alexander the Great couldn't go...the Navel of the Universe. Once again, Alexander tried to go through the Khyber Pass, which would've given him a route east that was north of the Himalayas. In failure, he turned back south to go through India, a strategy that bled his mighty army dry. But what about Plan A?

I speculate that his goal might've been Mount Kailash. Remember how Alexander fixated on religious centers like Egypt, Jerusalem, and Babylon. Like Hitler, he was obsessed with this "old kingdom" concept which manifested itself in the restoration of Nimrod's Esagila, the House of the Raised Head. For some reason, Alexander believed that whatever he found in the east would make all the bloodshed worth it. Hitler tried another tactic. Once he rose to power (and before he revealed his evil plan), he sent Ahnenerbe research teams into the region.

Their purpose?

The DNA trail of these superbeing Aryans. Now, I'm not German nor an expert in Mythology, but if you believe in Hyperborea, you believe in Atlantis, a different title for the same story. Here's the basics. Atlas was a titan who ruled his island nation. In the legend, this tall god-like-hero battled mere mortals from Greece. The poor Greeks didn't put up much of a fight. BUT! The gods decided to destroy Atlantis, scattering the people to wind. The sons of Atlas were also god-like-heroes, and two of them are of great interest to me. Iapetus, for example, has dozens and dozens of cross-over stories with Japheth, the son of Noah. Japheth went on to be the forefather of European nations. Another son was Hyas, which has an etymology in our word Asia. So what's Hitler doing sending scientists East? Well, if the

European DNA has been tainted by "lesser races" then perhaps we'll find better DNA with the descendants of Hyas. It's crazy stuff but darkly fascinating.

Unfortunately, the German scientists didn't find tall, blonde-haired, blue-eyed ancestors in Tibet, but they did return to Germany with some ancient knowledge. Remember, Helena Blavatsky returned from Tibet with her *Secret Doctrine* version of Gnosticism. What did the Nazi scientists return with?

Swastikas.

As the spiritual center of four world religions, Mount Kailash is also known as seven swastika mountain. Now, depending on which History Channel episode you watched, there are dozens of alternative facts involving the origin of the Swastika, but this one has teeth. Not only did the Swastika become the symbol of the Nazis, but guess what were the three primary colors for the walls of Atlantis? Red, White, and Black. The old Germanic myths and legends already in place were modified to incorporate the rediscovered Aryan lore.

You don't call it the Third Reich if you expect to be dead within a decade. For Hitler and his Nazi allies, who believed he was their long-awaited Messiah, they believed they were setting up something that would last. By this time, Eckhart was dead and replaced by Himmler, who set up Wewelsburg Castle as the center of their new world order. Some of Hitler's early conquests (which fueled George Lucas's imagination) were to obtain religious relics. One of the most interesting was the Spear of Destiny held in Austria. Hitler then turned his pseudo-scientist to finding the truth behind the Holy Grail.

Hmm? Where did that lead? Oh well.

Every kid in history class now knows it was Nazi vs. Jew during WWII, which led to millions dying during the Holocaust. I'm certainly not disputing this fact. Because of a few prophetic interpretations I hold, I do want to bring up that the Jews in central Europe are predominantly Ashkenazi Jews, whose migration into eastern Europe likely began in France. We'll get back to this loose string in the final chapter.

Yet along with targeting the Jews, Hitler's SS also targeted two very interesting groups: Gypsies and Freemasons. Freemasons? This makes a bit of sense if you're trying to not only eliminate secret societies that have lasted for centuries but also have legendary connections to the Holy Grail. Dang, Adolf. Freemasons are usually educated movers and shakers in society, and in the most modern definition, open to liberty and quite democratic. Guess who three of the most powerful Freemasons were when Hitler changed his philosophy? Henry Ford, Winston Churchill, and Franklin Roosevelt. Talk about picking a fight! At one point, though, Henry Ford supported Hitler's rise to power. Heck Ford even supported the Eugenics program borrowed by the Nazis to create the Master Race. Yet Hitler turns against his former allies? What did he learn?

Gypsies, on the other end of society, were typically poor outsiders. Yes, like Freemasons, they kinda operated independently of any nation, so that is a possible reason to be threated by this "underground" class of people. Was it personal for Hitler? Or was it Philosophical? The lore behind the Gypsies first brings them back to Romania, where the name Romani comes from. The name Gypsy? Depending on which historian you ask, that word has connections back to Egypt. Yet scientifically, we now understand that the Romani people originally began in the shadows of the Himalayas (Punjab region). To a nut like Hitler, this might've been some sort of Ayran connection.

Stopping the End of the World

I'm going to wrap up my chapter on Hitler with an outlandish theory. This isn't Biblical or historical. This theory is from a creative writer looking for good character motivation.

With all the crazies like Eckhart and Himmler proclaiming Hitler to be the long-awaited Messiah, it seems as if he believed it. Yet when you look at the other "heads," remember that they weren't clueless or atheist. They knew about God and defied him. My list of Lamech, Nimrod, Ramses, Alexander, Antiochus, and Domitian all knew God and the prophecies yet tried to thwart Him/it. Well, how would Hitler react when he found out he was part of team Perdition? With Catholic and Lutheran heritage, he likely knew the story long before he ascribed to the ANTI version of it espoused by Blavatsky and Company. If he knew he fit the parameters of being the "7th Head" and was fated to have a short rule before the arrival of the Antichrist and the End of the World, doesn't it make sense he would fight that prophecy?

How would you stop it from happening?

Eliminate the Holy Grail.

Eliminate the bloodline.

Eliminate those protecting the "Once and Future King."

If Hitler could kill the right family tree, he could crush the prophecy and give humanity a Third Reich. My theory is that Hitler targeted the Freemasons, Gypsies, and Jews not only because of the Master Race theories but because he worried more about stopping the Prophet from being born than the Antichrist from being made.

We'll get back to Hitler's likely fear of the Prophet in the final chapter.

First, let's wrap up some loose ends about $5+1+1=7=8$.

CHAPTER ELEVEN

MIXING THEM ALL TOGETHER

Two hundred years ago, in a friendly writing competition, author Mary Shelley tried to create the most horrifying tale imaginable. She won the bet with her tale ***Frankenstein.*** The tale describes how a scientist doesn't quite create life from scratch (that's God level stuff) but instead takes the pieces of dead guys, mixes them all together, and creates an abomination. In the story, the true monster was Dr. Frankenstein. Mary Shelley's nightmare was that as humans: if we aspire then we can reach. Dr. Frankenstein crossed the lines. His monster turned out to be better than normal humans: bigger, smarter, and far more passionate, which turned to wickedness and murder as he kills his creator. Oh, my, Mary.

Three thousand years earlier, Nebuchadnezzar shared the same dream as Mary Shelley. He dreamed that humanity would one day create an evil out of the parts of other evil men to make (muh, ha, ha), the ultimate evil in the galaxy. Our warnings about the Antichrist seem to predict an Antichrist monster.

Or…I could be wrong about all of this. I admit that it's some pretty far-fetched stuff. My theory is largely based on verb tenses: was, is, will be. Ultimately, it won't matter. The Antichrist will show up and do his thing. Don't forget his Prophet, either. These two are showing up soon and it doesn't really matter whom their kings were (if that theory is even correct).

Yet there is a reason why the prophecies were given.

And the way they were given? I think that matters too.

So let's recap before digging deeper into my theory.

Perhaps the earliest known End Times theory came from Enoch, who not only walked with God but also saw two cataclysms: the water and the fire. Now, it's tough to know how much of our modern version of Enoch to trust, right? Peter brings up Enoch's prophecy:

> **[2 Peter 1]: This second epistle, beloved, I now write unto you; in both which I stir up your pure minds by way of <u>remembrance</u>: [2] That ye may be mindful of the words which were spoken before by <u>the holy prophets</u>, and of the commandment of us the apostles of the Lord and Savior: [3] Knowing this first, that there shall come in the last days scoffers, walking after their own lusts, [4] And saying, Where is the promise of his coming? for since the fathers fell asleep, all things continue as they were from the beginning of the creation. [5] For this they willingly are ignorant of, that by the word of God the heavens were of old, and the earth standing out of the water and in the water: [6] Whereby the world that then was, being overflowed with <u>water, perished</u>: [7] But the heavens and the earth, which are now, by the same word are**

**kept in store, <u>reserved unto fire</u> against the day of judgment
and <u>perdition</u> of ungodly men.**

So here is Peter connecting the flood and the fire. I believe
he's got a good reason to do that. Peter brings up the flood again
when he talks about the evil of those days and how God still
managed to pull out 8 people in the last hour:

**[1 Peter 3]: when once the longsuffering of God waited in the
days of Noah, while the ark was a preparing, wherein few, that
is, eight souls were saved by water.**

Peter likely remembers the "Days of Noah" comparison
from the time he heard Jesus compare the two eras:

**Luke 17:26 And as it was in the days of Noah, so shall it be also
in the days of the Son of man.**

Earlier in this book, I talked about triggers for the End
Times. Quite obviously, the big boom of the Sixth Seal will her-
ald the Antichrist, which is when that 3.5ish year countdown
begins. But as I've shown, supervillains are not unique. We've
had several Antichrists between the first and the last, huh?
We've also had plenty of violence, haven't we? Yet in the Days
of Noah, the most unique feature of the flood was the Nephilim.

**[Genesis 6:1] And it came to pass, when men began to multiply
on the face of the earth, and daughters were born unto them,
[2] That <u>the sons of God</u> saw the <u>daughters of men</u> that they
were fair; and they took them wives of all which they chose. [3]
And the LORD said, My spirit shall not always strive with man,
for that he also is flesh: yet his days shall be an hundred and
twenty years. [4] There were <u>giants</u> in the earth in those days;
and also after that, when the sons of God came in unto the**

daughters of men, and they <u>bare children</u> to them, the same became mighty men which were of old, men of renown.

Again, many Christians do not subscribe to the most EPIC version of this passage since it's a bit embarrassing in a modern world: Giants. Go ahead and ignore that word. What are we left with? Group A breeds with Group B to produce Group C. God made Group A, and God certainly made Group B (men), but He did not make Group C. Group C is an abomination. Beginning with a flood and going all the way past Nimrod to Ramses and Moses, God goes out of his way to eliminate Giants. My theory?

Genetics.

This is the final straw that breaks the camel's back. This is the abomination that once again makes God hit the reset button. Last time, he used water. Next time, he'll use fire. What's so offensive? DNA makes us unique. Each person's genetic code spells out physical and behavioral traits. The billion little strands hold so much information, and quite likely, hold secrets we don't even understand yet. Whether a radish or a Russian, this DNA code is the blueprint for our design. While genetic code can modify from generation to generation, (we'll skip a discussion on evolution), it's a natural process. It's a Godly process.

Back in the days of Noah, the "sons of god" created abominations. Today, rogue scientists can create abominations to make something that God did not intend to exist. That's a major violation. That's a final straw.

Expressing outrage at genetic engineering would be hard to explain to modern humans let alone humans who lived thousands of years ago, but the visuals given to us seem pretty clear:

A seven headed dragon...that's not natural.

Animals with traits from other animals…that's not natural.

A man made up of pieces from other men…that's not natural.

A man being made up of 7 dead kings…that's not natural.

See the pattern?

Even though Daniel and Nebuchadnezzar knew nothing about chromosomes, they were freaked out by the monster-man described in Daniel 2. I feel there is a great clue hidden in the details of this passage. After all the symbolism about kingdoms, we get this phrase:

> **[Daniel 2:43] And whereas thou sawest iron mixed with miry clay, they shall mingle themselves with the seed of men: but they shall not cleave one to another, even as iron is not mixed with clay.**

Ew…seed. Yep. How's the monster-man of Daniel 2 going to be assembled? With the seed of men. Now ignoring the literal adhesive quality of, you know, this glue is symbolic. We know from John that the seven kings will be dead before the arrival of the 8th. Dead guys can't offer their seed. So why bother using this metaphor? The seed of men is a good way to explain to a 600 BC audience that the monster-man will be created by the stuff inside of the seed…the genetic code.

Look again how John describes his monster-man.

> **[Revelation 17:7] And the angel said unto me, Wherefore didst thou marvel? I will tell thee the mystery of the woman, and of the beast that carrieth her, which hath the seven heads and ten horns.[8] The beast that thou sawest was, and is not; and shall ascend out of the bottomless pit, and go into perdition: and they that dwell on the earth shall wonder, whose names were not written in the book of life from the foundation of the world,**

when they behold the beast that <u>was, and is not, and yet is</u>. **[9] And here is the mind which hath wisdom. The seven heads are seven mountains, on which the woman sitteth. [10] And there are seven kings: five are fallen, and one is, and the other is not yet come; and when he cometh, he must continue a short space. [11] And the beast that was, and is not, even <u>he is the eighth</u>, and is <u>of the seven</u>, and goeth into perdition. [12] And the ten horns which thou sawest are ten kings, which have received no kingdom as yet; but receive power as kings one hour with the beast. [13] These have <u>one mind</u>, and shall give their power and strength unto the beast.**

- <u>was, and is not; and shall</u> =the kings are from the past, present, and future.
- <u>bottomless pit</u>=yet they all die and descend to sheol (underworld).
- <u>not written in the book of life</u>=not normal humans, the Sons of Perdition.
- <u>he is the eighth</u>=the Frankenstein Antichrist, the Scary One
- <u>of the seven</u>=made up of the seven=
- of <u>one mind</u>=a genetic hybrid with one consciousness. The DNA guides him.

I just can't unsee what I've seen. I can't unread what I've read. I can't unthink what I've thunk. I'd love to diminish my concept of the Antichrist and make it just some random guy, but Biblical text (both OT and NT) goes to great length to make it more complicated than that. Again, in my early years, I was obsessed with genetics and DNA, so applying the concept to these verses frightens me a bit. As Mary Shelley speculated, hoping for moral scientists is problematic when humanity frequently crosses the line out of curiosity. The whole forbidden fruit metaphor works well. I'm going to stop arguing the case and apply the theory to some other verses about the Antichrist.

So how would this theory even work?

Four thousand years ago, this theory would have been unimaginable. Four hundred years ago, scientists were still dabbling in alchemy. Forty years ago...oh, heck yeah. In the 1980s, genetic research exploded in the laboratory, and in pop culture, we suddenly had updated horror stories involving cloning and bringing dinosaurs back from extinction. Science played it dumb in public, with Dolly the Sheep getting attention. Biotechnology students at Mankato State, for example, could imagine careers turning cauliflower plants goofy colors by flipping a few chromosomes around. But somewhere, the talented scientists were rolling up their sleeves. Somewhere, the boundaries were being pushed.

Scientifically, I believe we could pull off this crazy theory.

What about the archeology?

Yes, we need Indiana Jones for that part, don't we? We'd need DNA samples of each of the seven kings, so let's look to see if it would even be possible.

Antichrist Soup Shopping List

#7—Adolf Hitler: So after shooting himself in his head, he was found in that Berlin bunker and the world was told the news. What happened to the body? Oh, we lost it. My bad! Seriously? Now, this led to crazy theories about Hitler living, but that's not where I'm going. I'm assuming he really did shoot himself in the head, but then—somebody kept the body. This allows us to get a sample of DNA, doesn't it? Even without the body, we have enough "stuff" of Hitler to get DNA samples in other manners. American forces could've boxed up stuff at the Eagle's Nest of Wewelsburg Castle. DNA from Hitler is pretty easy.

#6—Domitian: My biggest concern with this one is that Romans loved to burn their leaders in great funeral pyres. Most historians believe he was cremated after the inglorious end of his reign. But remember, he was "out of favor" and would not receive honors. So yes, there are theories about his body being retrieved by his childhood nurse, who likely did the honors of cremation. But remember that Domitian did not worship the "modern" Roman gods. He worshiped the old school gods. Ah, this gets slippery quickly. I did a quick Google search and guess what the first three words given to me by our AI monster: This lost monument. Seriously! His tomb is lost. Slippery stuff. So Domitian's DNA is suspicious.

#5—Antiochus Epiphanes: He had a noted death but his burial is pretty obscure. His son did become the new king, so we can assume that evil dad was buried in the family crypts, likely in the capital city of Antioch. Unfortunately, the kid didn't rule for more than just a few years before a distant relative seized the throne for himself. Shortly after, the Romans and Parthians gobbled up the kingdom. So we'd need the best from Indiana Jones to track down this tomb. Antiochus Epiphanes's DNA is obscure.

#4—Alexander the Great: This one's a mystery. After his sudden death (likely Cassander), his family was wiped out (Cassander), and his restoration project of Esagila was demolished

(Cassander). Despite his very specific burial plans, Alexander's golden coffin was hijacked enroute to Egypt and vanished, leaving countless theories. Quite obviously, Alexander's allies knew his legacy was under attack, so somebody somewhere knows where the body was hidden. It's almost like Alexander knew his DNA would be important one day. Alexander's DNA is hidden.

#3—Ramses the Great: Got it. While the Egyptian Pharaohs thought they were being sneaky by burying their corpses under massive stone pyramids, humans have a way of figuring stuff out. During the 18th Dynasty, these New Order Egyptians, without direct ties to the previous dynasties, relied on caves near Thebes. So we have the preserved mummy of Ramses, which told scientists that he even had reddish hair (A descendant of Tantalus?). Ramses the Great's DNA is in a museum.

#2—Nimrod: This one is probably the most problematic since this was almost 4,000 years ago. While some of his peers in Egypt made tombs to endure, ancient Babylon got conquered a whole bunch of times. Speculatively, I like to picture Alexander the Great searching for it, but I have no connection in reality. For this to work, I'd need ancient tomb-raiders to collect this corpse and put it in a safer place than Babylon. Nimrod's DNA is lost.

#1—Lamech: This one is fun. Why fun? The flood. In concept, Lamech's city and kingdom got washed away in the Great Flood, and if you accept any of the specific details listed in Genesis, we're talking a cataclysmic, planet-scouring brillo pad of death. No one has a clue where anything was located before the flood. That would take some genius-level Solomon wisdom…oh, wait. Like Nimrod, Hitler, and Alexander went looking for traces of the "Old World," Solomon was also seeking for similar details. According to legend (not really Biblical stuff), Solomon sent his guys out on a treasure hunt to the corners of the world prior to building the Temple. This crazy time period resulted in tales of the shamir, the demon Asmodeus, and a magical ring. My point? Folks 3,000 years ago might've had a better idea of the "Old World" geography than we do today. A hidden kingdom with a hidden tomb? We'd need an Indiana Jones dialed up to 10.

My theory might work better in a novel (***The Alchemist's Tomb***), but with organized bad guys (remember the Gnostics?), there is a chance of this theory working. Of course, we might not need DNA. I have another theory (***The Dreamcatcher Chronicles),*** that explores the idea of all seven antichrists descending to the bottomless pit. Guess that means they're dead, huh Captain Obvious? Well, when #8 is "of the seven" and yet "these have one mind," it makes me think they have some sort of spiritual mental connection like dead Obiwan Kenobi had with Luke Skywalker.

So yes, the DNA hybrid monster has big problems to overcome, but thanks to the efforts of Ancestry DNA23 and Me, we might not need an archeologist much longer.

And the World Worships

Walking it back, it doesn't matter if I went 7 for 7 on my candidates or 0/7. The most dangerous aspect of the Frankenchrist is what would happen to our cultures. Despite Satan's best efforts, Christianity started as a spark and turned into a wildfire that spread across the world. Whether organic or nefarious, other religions always competed with first Judaism and then Christianity to keep humans from a healthy relationship with God. With the Frankenchrist, who needs God? Who needs faith when you have immortality?

Take a look at the reaction to the Antichrist:

[Rev 13:3] And I saw one of his heads as it were wounded to <u>death</u>; and his deadly wound was <u>healed</u>: and all <u>the world wondered</u> after the beast. [4] And they worshiped the dragon which gave power unto the beast: and <u>they worshiped</u> the beast, saying, Who is like unto the beast? who is able to make war with him? [5] And there was given unto him a mouth speaking great things and blasphemies; and power was given unto him to continue forty and two months. [6] And he opened his mouth in <u>blasphemy against God</u>, to blaspheme his name, and his tabernacle, and them that dwell in heaven.

<u>Death:</u> Only a celebrity (quite dead) would work for this magic trick. The world needs to be familiar with this person. It can't be some insignificant farmer or carpenter. It'll likely be one of the seven kings. Oh, and to impress the folks who might use the "mostly dead" card, pick somebody that's been dead for a while.

<u>Healed</u>: Too many "I saw a tunnel" candidates. This can't be somebody who flatlined on the operating table. Heck, my dad saw his own heart flatline and witnessed the ER personnel grab the paddles and shock his heart to restart beating. Stuff like that happens. To impress any scoffer and skeptic, you'll need a candidate that is VERY dead.

<u>Wondered</u>: Pick a king, any king. Ramses the Great? Okay, so we clone Ramses. Is it more impressive to make an adult clone or an infant clone? Adult clone. But here's the rub. Making a photocopy of you or your dog Fido is cool science but it

doesn't eliminate your fear of death. We don't want to be gone when we die. We want to come back. If scientists cloned Ramses, used 3D printers to build all the parts according to the DNA blueprint, and zapped him back to life…and he drooled like a newborn. Who would care? But if he woke to consciousness and could write Hieroglyphics, DANG…!!!! That's really Ramses.

<u>Worshiped:</u> Why would you need God if scientists could restore your DNA and bring your consciousness with it. Why would Muslims need Allah? Most religions are built on the concept that there will be judgment or reward in the afterlife. Well, with cloning & consciousness, baseball's Ted Williams could be cloned and know how to hit homeruns. Imagine the Red Sox farm system with a team full of Ted Williams clones.

<u>Blasphemy against God:</u> Science would eliminate the need to worship God. Carpe Diem. Seize the day. If it makes you happy, do it. Why pay for health insurance when $19.99 could get you cloning insurance. We'll bring you back and you can get right back on that merry-go ride. For..ev…er.

Regardless of how you interpret all 7,777 prophecies about the End Times, an end to religions is coming thanks to the possibility of science and DNA. Moral codes? Sure. A belief in the afterlife or judgment? LOL. It won't matter with what is being described. Christ conquered death, but now we can patent it and mass produce it. This will be our Tower of Babel. Just like God watched them stacking stones day after day, he's watching science get closer and closer to unlocking God's awesome creation—DNA—and using it against their Maker. The clock is ticking even before Perdition's great magic trick is revealed.

What the Theory Would Mean

Remember the metaphor of Jannes and Jambres vs Moses. Expect the bad guys to be able to pull off a miracle. The priests of Ramses were ready for their big day; they snapped their fingers and transformed their staffs into snakes (which were eaten, yes). The enemy is real, and the power of Perdition should not be underestimated. Expect the dark miracle.

But what led up to it?

So let's assume that scientists can create a genetic hybrid with the best (or worst) traits from these seven kings. We'd need motivated bad guys with a plan. Forget my "choices" for the seven heads—those names are irrelevant in the prophecy. We'd need bad guys who could access these old Kings. From the Gnostics like Helena Blavatsky to Hitler's fear of gypsies and Freemasons, we'd need some organized secret societies to be working on this audacious plan. For the Antichrist to show up immediately after the Sixth Seal, the planning needed to start long before I came up with the idea for a plot in my fictional novel series. Nimrod seemed to know about Lamech's Old Kingdom, Ramses knew the importance of protecting DNA, Alexander seemed to know about Nimrod, Antiochus seemed to know about how to wage war on God, and Hitler seemed to know "all of the above." My point? Gathering of the DNA needed to happen.

Then what?

Unlike Nebuchadnezzar's nightmare, we're not sewing body parts together. Four decades ago, the brightest and best genetic engineers needed to be hired for this special project since this will be a cutting edge project. If it were me, instead of sewing body parts together, I'd be weaving the genetic codes of the seven into one (8th) body to create the $5+1+1=7=8$ Antichrist. But...wouldn't you first test the theory. If you've got Alexander's DNA, why not make an Alexander clone. So in my crazy lab, we could have straight-up cloning going on at the same time you're making your hybrid. See how much fun it'd be to play mad scientist!

Opening the Gates of Hell

Normally, death is a one-way street. Christ flipped that idea on its head 2,000 years ago, but Beelzebub's time as gate-keeper has been unblemished since that day. Yet two clues given to us trouble me:

ascend out of the <u>bottomless pit</u>

These have <u>one mind</u>

Somehow, the one mind of the Antichrist will be fueled by the others, who quite obviously will "ascend" out of what we call hell. How does a soul "ascend" out of hell? Does Beelzebub open the gates for them? Is that the angel that "unlocks" them (Apollyon)? Oh, wait, we have a prime suspect, and I've saved him for the last chapter.

It's time to meet...the prophet.

THE BEAST FROM EARTH

Did you think I'd forget about him? The metaphors are interesting. Why is one beast "from the water" and the other "from the earth"? Yes, Satan has a ton of water dragon/leviathan references. Double yes, the "gates" of the down place are mostly described with watery descriptions (check out Jonah). So it makes sense for the Antichrist to come out of the sea when the 5+1+1 fellows have all died. Their souls need to be in the down place for them to "ascend" like it said in the previous chapter. The Antichrist is going to come up from the down place to rule.

But the other guy?

Oh, he's an earth metaphor. Why an earth metaphor? I think he's going to be born normally and naturally. His DNA is going to come from parents who are/were on the earth. Aside from being called the "Beast from Earth" he is also known as the Antichrist's prophet, and quite surprisingly, he has as much to do with the final years as the Antichrist. Let's read his introduction:

> **[Revelation 13:11] And I beheld another beast coming up out of the earth; and he had two horns <u>like a lamb</u>, and he spake as <u>a dragon</u>. [12] And he exercised all the power of the first beast before him, and causeth the earth and them which dwell therein to worship the first beast, whose deadly wound was healed. [13] And he doeth <u>great wonders,</u> so that he maketh fire come down from heaven on the earth in the sight of men, [14] And <u>deceiveth them</u> that dwell on the earth by the means of those miracles which he had power to do in the sight of the beast; saying to them that dwell on the earth, that they should make <u>an image to the beast</u>, which had the wound by a sword, and did live. [15] And he had <u>power to give life</u> unto the image of the beast, that the image of the beast should both speak, and cause that as many as would not worship the image of the beast should be killed.**

So let's look at the characteristics described:
- **<u>like a lamb</u>**=a pleasing form?
- **<u>a dragon</u>**=but speaks evil?
- **<u>great wonders</u>**=miracles and wonders make him a sorcerer of sorts
- **<u>deceiveth them</u>**=a false hero
- **<u>an image to the beast</u>**=a clone?
- **<u>power to give life</u>**=life returns to an empty body=clone?

I've heard the statue theory, but this is the 21st century where we have AI. Statues aren't going to fool anyone. The ability to play with a human marionette is much more impressive, and restoring a body to life is one thing but returning a soul…dang!

But this guy creates a religion. He's the speaker. He's the miracle worker. From the Sixth Seal all the way to Armageddon, this guy is bent on wiping out Christians. Who is he? Where does he come from?

While I strongly believe that the Abomination of Desolation is the Beast from Sea, who is likely manufactured through DNA, the other guy we just met is just as bad. In fact, I think we might need to examine some of those titles we read about earlier:

> **[2 Thessalonians 2:3] Let no man deceive you by any means: for that day shall not come, except there come a falling away first, and that <u>man of sin be revealed</u>, the <u>son of perdition</u>; [4] Who opposeth and exalteth himself above all that is called God, or that is worshiped; so that he as God sitteth in the temple of God, shewing himself that he is God. [5] Remember ye not, that, when I was yet with you, I told you these things? [6] And now ye know what withholdeth that <u>he might be revealed in his time</u>. [7] For the mystery of iniquity doth already work: only he who now letteth will let, until he be taken out of the way. [8] And then shall <u>that Wicked be revealed</u>, whom the Lord shall consume with the spirit of his mouth, and shall destroy with the brightness of his coming: [9] Even <u>him, whose coming is after the working of Satan with all power and signs and lying wonders</u>, [10] And with all deceivableness of unrighteousness in them that perish; because they received not the love of the truth, that they might be saved. [11] And for this cause God shall send them <u>strong delusion</u>, that they should <u>believe a lie</u>: [12] That they all might be damned who believed not the truth, but had pleasure in unrighteousness.**

In these verses, I suddenly began to wonder if we're talking about the Beast from Water or...the Beast from Earth. Our "prophet" could be the Man of Sin. Notice how this passage uses the word "revealed" three times. What's going on with that? To be revealed, you need to be hidden, don't you? Yes, my theory of DNA could work here. A secret DNA project could suddenly be revealed. Yet I think there might be some meaning in the symbol of "Beast from Earth" rather than "sea."

Remember, I go down rabbit holes with my obsessions. I'm always trying to bring meaning where there might not be any meaning. If a verse doesn't make sense to me, it'll fester until I can make it jive with the other theories.

We need to talk about Judas.

The Son of Perdition

As I mentioned earlier, Team Evil is much more complicated than just Team Satan. You have armies of demons, 4 fallen angels, Apollyon, Mr. Sea and Mr. Earth, Satan, Death, and Hades. I've speculated that Perdition is likely something far more sinister than Satan since he's likely either Death or Hades as 1 of the 2 final enemies. Sons of Perdition, Sons of Belial, and Many Antichrists can be seen throughout the Old Testament, yet Jesus says something quite chilling during the Last Supper scene.

Let me recap. Dusk. The Upper Room. The Lamb Day has just begun. Sometime during the evening, Judas Iscariot ducks out after being slyly identified by Jesus to John. Then Jesus thanks God for giving him disciples. That's when Jesus says this:

[John 17:6] I have manifested thy name unto the men which thou gavest me out of the world: thine they were, and thou gavest them me; and they have kept thy word. [7] Now they

have known that all things whatsoever thou hast given me are of thee. [8] For I have given unto them the words which thou gavest me; and they have received them, and have known surely that I came out from thee, and they have believed that thou didst send me. [9] I pray for them: I pray not for the world, but for them which thou hast given me; for they are thine. [10] And all mine are thine, and thine are mine; and I am glorified in them. [11] And now I am no more in the world, but these are in the world, and I come to thee. Holy Father, keep through thine own name those whom thou hast given me, that they may be one, as we are. [12] While I was with them in the world, I kept them in thy name: those that thou gavest me I have kept, and none of them is lost, <u>but the son of perdition</u>; that the scripture might be fulfilled.

Paraphrased: You gave me 11 disciples. I didn't lose any of them. Judas doesn't count because he is the son of perdition. I never lost something I never had. Judas was born evil.

Whoa…Jesus just connected Judas to being a son of Perdition, and that festered in me for years. As a child, I saw movies that portrayed Judas as jealous, petty, greedy, etc. He showed human emotions and even repentance when he hung himself over guilt. In a way, it was hard to differentiate him from the denial of Peter. Yet here's Jesus calling him the son of Perdition.

Mind you, there are other really bizarre "evil" phrases used earlier in the Last Supper scene. Don't forget when "Satan entered into Judas" (Luke 22:3) and "Satan entered into him" (John 13:27). Say what? Granted, Judas likely wasn't spinning his head and vomiting pea soup, but two accounts describe a possession by one of the biggest players on Team Evil. So not only do you have a Son of Perdition reference but you also have a strange alliance with Satan.

When did Judas stop being possessed by Satan? Remember: he immediately goes to the priests to arrange for the arrest. That's Satan. He accompanies a detachment of soldiers (upwards of 500) with plans to crush Christianity at the Mount of Olives. That's Satan. However, before they get to the Mount of Olives, Jesus steps out of the Garden of Gethsemane and turns himself in, saving the crowd on the Mount of Olives. With a kiss, Jesus is betrayed by a trusted friend. That's Satan. Jesus just foiled Satan's plan to crush Christianity on the Mount of Olives, and when Satan realizes he's been duped, he (and Judas) tries to give the money back to stop the sham trial. Why?

Cuz Jesus wants the trial!

Unfortunately, nobody will listen to Judas, who they assume has cold feet, but remember…that's Satan. If Satan is panicking about his failed plan, to stop it, he'd need to be let out of Judas and…oh, yeah…Judas hangs himself. That's Satan?

Huh…(we'll get back to this in a few pages).

It seems that like the Antichrist, Judas had some impressive connections. So let's look closer at Judas.

The Man from Kerioth

Not much to say about Judas Iscariot (Is-Cariot=from Kerioth). We don't get any good anecdotes about how they met. He doesn't have any interesting stories. He's chosen from the crowd as 1 of the 12 followers, yet at the Last Supper, we find out that not only was he a thief and traitor, but that he was a Son of Perdition.

The aftermath of the betrayal is discussed in Acts, when they have to pick a replacement for Judas on the team of 12.

[Acts 1:5] And in those days Peter stood up in the midst of the disciples, and said, (the number of names together were about an hundred and twenty,) [16] Men and brethren, this scripture must needs have been fulfilled, which the Holy Ghost by the mouth of David spake before concerning Judas, which was guide to them that took Jesus. [17] For he was numbered with us, and had obtained part of this ministry. [18] Now this man purchased a field with the reward of iniquity; and falling headlong, he burst asunder in the midst, and all his bowels gushed out. [19] And it was known unto all the dwellers at Jerusalem; insomuch as that field is called in their proper tongue, Aceldama, that is to say, The field of blood.

Gross. Violent. (And may I speculate:) That's Satan. That might've been the end of the story for most, but Peter makes a very wild connection in the next verse. He officially goes on record to say that Judas was involved in an Old Testament prophecy. Peter (not Jason Lee Willis) brings up a specific prophecy and stamps his interpretation right on it by saying: "That's Judas." Curious? First, here's what Peter said in Acts:

[20] For it is written in the book of Psalms, Let his habitation be desolate, and let no man dwell therein: and his bishoprick let another take.

Here's the passage in Psalms 109:

Song of the Slandered
[1] {To the chief Musician, A Psalm of David.} Hold not thy peace, O God of my praise; [2] For the mouth of the wicked and the mouth of the deceitful are opened against me: they have spoken against me with a lying tongue. [3]They compassed me about also with words of hatred; and fought against me without a cause. [4] For my love they are my adversaries: but I give myself unto prayer. [5] And they have

rewarded me evil for good, and hatred for my love. [6] Set thou a wicked man over him: and let Satan stand at his right hand. [7] When he shall be judged, let him be condemned: and let his prayer become sin. [8] Let his days be few; and <u>let another take his office</u>. [9] Let his children be fatherless, and his wife a widow. [10] Let his children be continually vagabonds, and beg: let them seek their bread also out of their desolate places. [11] Let the extortioner catch all that he hath; and let the strangers spoil his labor. [12] Let there be none to extend mercy unto him: neither let there be any to favor his fatherless children. [13] Let his posterity be cut off; and in the generation following let their name be blotted out. [14] Let the iniquity of his fathers be remembered with the LORD; and let not the sin of his mother be blotted out.

[15] Let them be before the LORD continually, that he may cut off the memory of them from the earth. [16] Because that he remembered not to show mercy, but persecuted the poor and needy man, that he might even slay the broken in heart. [17] As he loved cursing, so let it come unto him: as he delighted not in blessing, so let it be far from him. [18] As he clothed himself with cursing like as with his garment, so let it come into his bowels like water, and like oil into his bones. [19] Let it be unto him as the garment which covereth him, and for a girdle wherewith he is girded continually. [20] Let this be the reward of mine adversaries from the LORD, and of them that speak evil against my soul.

Verse 21 is the turn where David asks for strength in dealing with evil, so I'll stop there, but DANG! That's a lot to unpack.

In verse 8, you've got the Peter connection to Judas. According to Peter, the HIM=Judas. That's on the record. So let's review this with Judas in mind as the antecedent to David's vague prayer.

let his prayer become sin=this guy can fake being a good disciple, but his works are evil. As the son of Perdition, this guy was born bad.

his days be few=Judas dies as a young man. While it never says, he's an angry young man.

Satan stand at his right hand=we're coming back to this one, but notice how this phrase implies that Satan assists him. Again, I believe that Perdition outranks Satan in the playing deck of evil cards. When Luke and John bring up that Satan possessed Judas, it fulfills this prophecy.

Let his children be fatherless=Sorry about this, but we're going down this rabbit hole for the rest of the chapter. Judas had kids? The grandchildren of Perdition? Judas turned out to be an unholy villain, and despite the best intentions of forgiving Christians, these kids would not be safe in Israel after this betrayal. Wow, kids? You'll see why this intrigues me shortly.

his wife a widow=So Mrs. Iscariot… If I didn't read so much mythology and lore, this one wouldn't go anywhere, but I'll come back to her also.

let their name be blotted out=here's where things get curious. Yes, being born from Perdition likely means you're not written down in the Book of Life. Sorry kids. That's the most obvious "sins of the father" metaphor here. HOWEVER…blotting out implies covering up or hiding. The kids didn't die. What happened? They vanished.

children be continually vagabonds=vagabond implies wandering, so this clue seems to imply that not only did they go underground but they had to stay on the run. Did they go someplace far, far away? I'm betting so. "Continually" also seems to imply that this wasn't a brief experience. The bloodline of Judas stays on the run from generation to generation to generation.

Let the iniquity of his fathers be remembered=Sins of Judas's fathers? Plural? Mother is singular yet father is plural. Surely this means forefathers or something. Yet I'm left with the curiosity about who Judas's fathers were.

let not the sin of his mother be blotted out=Centuries before Judas was born, David wrote a poem about evils of JI's mom. Why? Isn't betraying the Christ enough? Why bring up mom? She must be impressively wicked to warrant a line in David's poem.

before the LORD continually=Here we go again. Continually is mentioned again. The implication is that this "curse" will not be lifted quickly. Remember, the Sins of the Father goes for seven generations, right? What about betraying the Son of God? Dang…

from the earth=and there it is…Beast from Earth. As I mentioned earlier, spirits have a watery connection throughout the Old Testament. The prophet, however, will have an active bloodline. I speculate that this Son of Perdition will have a connection going all the way back to Judas.

come into his bowels=What are the odds, huh? There is a reason why the description of Judas's death included guts.

oil into his bones=A curious phrase. Yes, it seems to fit the "infected with evil" metaphor, yet considering the "possession" incident with Satan, I think it could be a metaphor for that also.

the garment which covereth him=like a mask. The bad guys thought they were being sneaky by sending Judas into the midst to thwart God's plans. Being good was a facade. OR…Satan entering him is the garment that covered him.

So this little reference by Peter opens a whole can of worms, doesn't it (sorry about the bowels pun). The story of Judas was not over. His parents got mentioned, his wife got mentioned, and his kids…don't get me started with the kids.

Psalm 41 is also cited in connection with Judas. While David seems to focus on the Christ rather than the Betrayer, it's another moment where he's reflecting on the prophecy almost a thousand years before it arrives"

[Psalm 42:1] {To the chief Musician, A Psalm of David.} Blessed is he that considereth the poor: the LORD will deliver him in time of trouble. [2]The LORD will preserve him, and keep him alive; and he shall be blessed upon the earth: and thou wilt not deliver him unto the will of his enemies.[3] The LORD will strengthen him upon the bed of languishing: thou wilt make all his bed in his sickness. [4] I said, LORD, be merciful unto me: heal my soul; for I have sinned against thee. [5] Mine enemies speak evil of me, When shall he die, and his name perish? [6] And if he come to see me, he speaketh vanity: his heart gathereth iniquity to itself; when he goeth abroad, he telleth it. [7] All that hate me whisper together against me: against me do they devise my hurt. [8] An evil disease, say they, cleaveth fast unto him: and now that he lieth he shall rise up no more.[9] Yea, mine own familiar friend, in whom I trusted, which did eat of my bread, hath lifted up his heel against me. [10] But thou, O LORD, be merciful unto me, and raise me up, that I may requite them.[11] By this I know that thou favourest me, because mine enemy doth not triumph over me. [12] And as for me, thou upholdest me in mine integrity, and settest me before thy face forever.

[13] Blessed be the LORD God of Israel from everlasting, and to everlasting. Amen, and Amen.

Again, this one is just the "trusted friend," but considering the lack of backstory for Judas Iscariot and the whole "Satan entered him" details, and here with the "heel" imagery from the Garden of Eden punishments, it makes me wonder if it's not Judas—but Satan—who was once the trusted friend.

W.W.J.D?

What would Judas do?

Why did Judas do it?

Movie producers love humanizing Judas, but according to Jesus, the man was a Son of Perdition and was NEVER good. He was a Man of Sin.

Yet this phrase comes up again in Thessalonians 2:3 that the End Times won't begin until the Man of Sin is revealed:

[Thessalonians 2:3] Let no man deceive you by any means: for that day shall not come, except there come a falling away first, and that man of sin be revealed, the son of perdition;

This could totally be the Antichrist. Following the epic devastation of Seal #6, the world will need a heroic leader to help fix things up. Plus, you'll also have the pseudoscience-supernatural resurrection that'll really impress people. The world will marvel. Yet if my theory is correct, the Antichrist will be Melchizedek-ish by not having any lineage. He's a test tube baby. A Frankenstein fabrication from Team Evil. What's to reveal? To reveal something, you've got to be hiding something, right?

With Jesus clearly establishing Judas=Son of Perdition, this verse could mean that the End Times won't come until JUDAS IS REVEALED. But Judas is dead, so….oh….his kids.

Back in 2006, I was just studying Psalm 109 when there was a ripple in the news cycle: the Gospel of Judas had been discovered and translated. Now, I already knew about the Gnostic texts that tried to poison and muddy First Century Christianity. Gnostics took the names of disciples and apostles and ruined the message. The story about Jesus marrying Mary Magdalene, for example, was a whopper of a tale. The Gnostics were and are our spiritual enemies.

So I was not seeking any truth from the Gospel of Judas when I learned about it. I assumed it was complete wickedness. I still feel that way. Yet…(Solomon moment here)…understanding our enemy is insightful. So I went down that rabbit hole (and I needed a spiritual shower after it).

The Gospel of Judas Revealed

Something can be old and true. Something can be old and a lie. When media outlets and news agencies learned a recently discovered text had just been translated, they trumpeted their horns and tried to sell it as the "original" Easter story, but it was just another Gnostic text. Most of Christianity ignored it as a fraud or a lie. That's cool.

Yet the Gnostics were real. This unearthed text is real. Granted, it's not from God. It's not penned by Judas since he hung himself. Yet Gnostics wrote it down and guarded it for a reason. So while the world largely ignored this "breaking news" event, I stuck my nose in it and realized how it not only gave evil insight into the events of Judas but it also gave a Gnostic plan for a nefarious concept: a hidden bloodline.

The setting is three days before Passover, so our Sunday or Monday (depending on how you figure the eight days. Is Passover the Lamb Day or Celebration Day?). Gnostic roles are often flip side, so instead of the real Jesus he gets a pseudo-Jesus. This figure is something akin to Perdition/Darkness/Belial and first attempts to deceive the other 11 disciples. Fail. So Perdition asks who has the strength to do something important? Judas steps up and recognizes Perdition as a spirit from Barbello (more Gnostic theology). Perdition then tells Judas that he will be replaced in the 12. Obviously, this upsets Judas, but Perdition sets up revenge. He describes how the final generation of humanity will be "strong and Holy" (quite the opposite of the evil described in Revelation). Perdition then adds that **"no host of angels of the stars will rule over them."** What does that mean? They are godless. Here's the pitch to Easter Week Judas: You can get your revenge over the 11 by agreeing to a plan that lets your offspring rule over humanity.

The text then dumps a bunch of Gnostic philosophies on Judas. Perdition talks smack about God and the evil he created with flesh and the physical world. Destroying flesh and the physical world will bring us closer to the original spiritual world, apparently. Perdition then spins reality and explains that the church being set up by Jesus will only lead to vile, evil priests. Forget 2,000 years of bringing salvation, Perdition tells Judas that the Church will **"lead you astray"** since the priests are filled with **"lawlessness & error."** Perdition wants the Church to be seen as pathetic. In looking back at the past 2,000 years, it's easy to see how EVIL did foreshadow a corrupt human institution. Every generation has evil religious leaders. Yet Perdition is the dark force corrupting men.

So who's to blame?

Then the text lays out more of the game plan for Team Judas. **"On the Last Day, they will be put to shame,"** which is a way of seeing the prophesied Apostasy, the falling away of the Church. Now motivated against the Church, Judas is taught the truth about "Sophia," the good spirit of wisdom and how each human has a Gnostic angel to guide them (cue Satan).

Apparently, Judas's current angel has led him astray and into believing the message of Jesus. Sucker! Perdition shows him a glimpse of Paradise but tells him he'll never be able to see it if he doesn't listen up closely. Then the text drops something right out of Psalm 109. Remember all the talk about Judas and his family? Well, get a load of this: **"Judas said, 'Master, could it be that my seed is under control of the rulers?' Perdition answered and said to him, 'Come, that I...but that you will grieve much when you see the kingdom and all its generation.' When he heard it, Judas said to him, 'What good is it that I have received it? For you have set me apart from that generation."**

Seed under control of the rulers? That line jumped off the page for me.

Perdition answers Judas with this promise: **"You will become the 13th, and you will be cursed by the other generations—and you will come to rule over them. In the last days, they will curse your ascent to the Holy**

Generation." Things get trippy for Judas, and he's shown some bizarre secrets of the Cosmos, and after, Perdition tells him how God is lying to us. Evil Fake News. Yet then another wild detail is tossed out in the next: there will be a **"divine Self-Generated"** figure.

Seriously!?!

That sounds like my Frankenstein Antichrist. There is also talk of 4 angels (fallen angels in Revelation 9:14?). Finally, Judas is shown a priestly Luminary who will lead this final generation. Um, can you say Judas Junior?

Again, after Dan Brown's Da Vinci Code became a #1 International Bestseller, I'd gone down the Gnostic rabbit hole a few years earlier, so when I read this text, I knew it was Bizzaro World where anything good was evil and anything evil was good.

Myriads of Angels=the 200,000 Demon Army

Incorruptible Generation=demons spirits of the Nephilim

12 Aeons=12 false gods of the underworld.

Like that!

Yet in the gobbledy-gook of Gnostic symbolism, it brings up 5 "beasts" and the 2 who were to come. Remember, this is supposedly happening in 33 AD. It appears as if Team Antichrist has a clear understanding of the 5+1+1=7=8 prophecy in Revelation before it is even written by John (Granted, this text coulda been written in 200 AD). Even so, Holy Cow! (sorry about the Baal pun).

The text concludes with some more wild evil prophecies. Perdition believes "The Generation" at the end times will live forever. If true, why wouldn't you make plans for an International Space Station, lunar bases, and a settlement on Mars? With DNA technology, robots, and space travel, you can avoid God's wrath by leaving the planet, right? This certainly explains why the Earth is scoured yet after a 1,000 years pass, the Armies of Gog and Magog appear out of nowhere (space?). Perdition then blames God for causing Adam to sin. Perdition mocks the Revelation predictions about Team Jesus winning. Then Perdition says, **"The Star that leads the way is Your Star."**

That's when Satan is given Judas. Satan once held the title Lucifer, the Morning Star. Why does Judas need help from Satan? To betray Jesus. This is how the text finishes: **"But you will exceed them (the other disciples). For you will sacrifice the man that clothes me."** Remember, this encounter began with Perdition taking on the familiar form of Jesus to trick Judas into a conversation.

And what a conversation they had.

The Holy Grail Legend

But the Gnostics are big, fat liars, right?

Unfortunately, my time in the rabbit hole left me with a few unsettling questions. A few years before the Gospel of Judas came out, I followed Dan Brown (the Da Vinci Code) guy down a historical rabbit hole. There was a method in this guy's madness. He'd thrown in bits of historical truth along with bits of fabrication. Heck, he didn't even invent his plot. What was his plot? Oh, his assertion is that Jesus and Mary Magdalene were lovers, and that after the crucifixion, MM took their child (a girl named Sarah) and fled the Holy Land. Thousands of years later, the lead female character turned out to be…the heir of Jesus.

Does Dan Brown really believe this? Doesn't matter. He just took some modern conspiracy theories and turned them into a page-turner that became very popular. There were several recent books that packaged it all together for Mr. Brown. The allure of the Dan Brown plot wasn't just a connection to old Gnostic texts but also a sprinkling of 2,000 years of historical conspiracy theories. Just because something is old doesn't mean it's true.

As I'm flipping through the pages, starring some details and crossing out others, I recognized where I'd seen some of these details: the King Arthur Legend. At the bottom of the King Arthur story is the concept of hiding a secret king whose identity has been hidden from the public so that he can one day assume the throne. Yes, Holy Grail means the cup of Christ, but Dan Brown also brings up the symbolic interpretation of the metaphor...a holy bloodline. Writers back in the day also noted a strange conspiracy theory and put a positive spin on it for jolly old England.

The surprising feature of the Holy Grail story in the Arthurian Legend is its connections to Christianity. Sure, there's plenty of pagan Dungeons and Dragons stuff, but that stuff is fun whereas the Christian stuff is actually the more disturbing aspect of the tale. To summarize, Joseph of Arimathea (Luke 23:49-53) who left the Holy Lands, traveled to distant England, and not only brought Christianity with him but he also brought the Holy Grail. Cool, huh? When you throw in a few knights like Percival and Lancelot, things get very complicated and suddenly there's talk about the Grail being kept in France also. Finding the Grail is a solemn oath for the Knights of the Round Table. There's nothing Biblical about this story AND there is nothing mentioned about the Holy Grail (Gnostic legends, remember).

Yet for more than a thousand years, folks could openly talk about the Holy Grail and the secret heir in public. Heck, it's just a story. Yet even amateur sleuths can dig around this legend and find connections to modern Freemasons, old school Templar Knights, and even older Merovingian Kings. Following Dan Brown and the modern theorist down this rabbit hole was entertaining, but at no time did I ever think Jesus had a secret heir. Even when they brought up details from the 1st century about a woman with a daughter named Sarah did I believe that—stop the presses! (I just read the Gospel of Judas!)

Suddenly the cover story connected to a new theory of mine.

Jesus didn't have a wife and child.

But Judas did.

St. Sarah la Kali

At the root of the Holy Grail legend is a curious, disturbing, and well-documented legend. Dan Brown and Company didn't just invent the name of Sarah Christ. It turns out that at the bottom of this legend there is a town in France that still celebrates an event that happened nearly two thousand years ago. In the seaside village of Saintes-Maries-de-la-Mer, they venerate Saint Sarah, who is known as the patron saint of displaced people. Sarah la Kali also means Sarah the Black, which is blatantly pointing out that she was a foreigner with Egyptian roots. In this local legend, displaced Jewish-Christians fled the Holy Lands in 42 AD.

Which ones?

While not Joseph of Arimathea, this group supossedly had Lazarus and his sisters. (Um, yeah, wasn't she named Mary?) In fact, the legend says there were three Marys with Lazarus. So without too much debate: yep, Mary Magdalene and a child named Sarah.

Wait! This legend seems familiar.

Oh, it should. Remember Hitler? (how could you forget). Remember his hatred of Jews? (of course). Remember who else he targeted for death camps? Freemasons and Gypsies.

Rabbit Hole #74: The Tribe of Benjamin turned to Belial/Baal worship.

Rabbit Hole #75: The 11 tribes almost wiped out the tribe of Benjamin

Rabbit Hole #76: The 11 tribes took Benjamin brides to keep the tribe alive.

Rabbit Hole #142: The Northern Tribes were assimilated by Assyria

Rabbit Hole #150: The tribes of Benjamin and Judah were taken to Babylon

Rabbit Hole #265: Turns out some Benjaminites settled in Greece and France

Rabbit Hole #298: Rome tried to erase Jewish culture from Israel post 70 AD

Rabbit Hole #364: Jewish refugees settled in communities scattered in Europe.

Rabbit Hole #396: The "Ashkenazi" Jew migration began in France before settling in central Europe.

Well, folks, each year in Saintes-Maries-de-la-Mer, thousands of Gypsies make a pilgrimage to this site, where they honor St. Sarah la Kali. Like the Jewish people, the Romani people are a nation living in unwalled villages throughout Europe. Long, long ago, they migrated from the region south of the Himalayas known as the Punjab region. You know: where Alexander brought his army. You're familiar with the Romani also: targeted by Hitler (after his scientists made the trip to the Himalayas).

Obviously, the Egyptian origins of Sarah were noted by the Romani people long ago, and for the past 2,000 years the Gypsy community revered her so much that the Catholic Church added her to the ever expanding list of saints. We'll get back to this "gyp" concept in a bit, but for now, I wanted to focus on another rabbit hole: Kali.

In my mythology studies (likely after watching *The Temple of Doom),* Kali is a major goddess in Indian lore, so that makes sense; however, I came across her name several other times in my research. Her ties? Ding, ding! Oh, yes, she has strong connections to Semiramis and Anath. With Anath, it is an even more striking connection. Both are bloody, violent, female warriors. Although most experts have no credible clue where the Hyksos people came from, I did come across a theory that they were displaced nomadic raiders of the 14th century BC who came out of...the Indus valley. So all the Baal and Anath worship could connect to Kali and Vishnu.

Getting back to Hitler, once he obtained power, he targeted Freemason groups, Gypsies, and Jews. If Dan Brown and other modern hacks were able to piece together the Holy Grail=Blood line theory, Hitler's Gnostic crazies certainly had better resources to get to the bottom of this legend.

How would this serve Hitler?

Well, if he wanted to challenge his fate as a "short time" leader, destroying the bloodline could keep the Prophet from ever being born. If he killed the right "hidden heir," the Third Reich would really be able to continue for a thousand years because the End Times prophecy would not bring an end to the world. Think of it like the Romans: "Let's do a census, right down all the names of the House of David, and if push comes to shove, we'll target the whole list for assassination (which is what Domitian decided to do). Like father, like son (or in this case: Like (Nimrod, Ramses, Domitian), like Hitler. We have to assume, the Freemason Alliance of Franklin Delano Roosevelt, Henry Ford, and Winston Churchill stopped Hitler from getting the right hidden heir.

Mother Egypt

When I started working on a book about the Magi, I quickly discovered I didn't have a clue about a global power of the day called Parthia. Parthia filled the map between India and Turkey (Iran+Iraq+a bunch of other territories). Since at least 1 of the Magi had to come "from the East" and likely the Bagdad/Babylon region, I went down this rabbit hole to learn. For my plot purposes, I didn't really get much out of it, but after my cookies and algorithms noted my new interest, suddenly, I was being shown related material. I found this book (sorry, I didn't take note. I had a PDF copy of it that was lost during a phone transfer) that proposes a fascinating theory. I poke around at the theory, and like me, a lot of historians scoffed at it, but that's what historians are good at. My point? I'm not sure how much I trust this next paragraph.

A generation before Jesus, a Roman by the name of Julius Caesar (oh, you know that name), ended up claiming Egypt for the Roman Empire. In Egypt, he met Cleopatra (know her too?) and ended up bringing her back to Rome as a trophy. So far, so good. The curious fact is that they had a love child named Musa. This gal grew up with the nickname of "The Italian Whore" which makes sense. She's half Italian and half Cleopatra-level-hot. Apparently, Cleopatra had other daughters, and one was given to Herod the Great for his help in defeating a rebellion led by Mark Anthony and Cleopatra (yes, the Shakespeare play). Back in Rome, Musa grew up and soon became an eligible maiden. A lot of this is unsubstantiated rumor (but there are entire books written on the subject).

However, historical records mention how Julius's adopted son Octavius (later Augustus) made a peace treaty with the Kingdom of Parthia. His offering? Musa. Now, history is based on all the official records, which claims she is an Italian slave girl. What kind of insult would that be? However, if she **was** indeed the biological heir of TWO powerful kingdoms (Egypt and Rome), that would sweeten the deal. So…Musa becomes the bride of Phraates IV, the ruler of Parthia.

And then it gets dark. (Really dark). Young Musa quickly becomes Phraates IV's favorite plaything and begins nudging the others out of the way. After she gives birth to her own son (Phraates V), she convinces the king to send his four other sons/heirs to Rome for education, leaving her son as the only heir. After 18 years of marriage, the Parthian historians believe she poisoned her husband. In 2 BC, she then takes the throne for herself. Not only does she take power as a foreigner but the coins minted during that era label her as (deep breath): Thea Musa Ourania, which translates to "Queen of Heaven."

In classic Semiramis fashion, she then strengthened the throne by (clearing throat) marrying her son. Ew! Josephus the Jewish historian goes into great length about this despite modern historians doubting the incestuous tales.

So the "Whore of Babylon" becomes an embarrassment to her subjects. The locals support a coup yet Musa manages to flee Parthia alive.

Now this is where it gets interesting.

The book I read (and lost) went away from the official record of Musa. With his Cleopatra theory, she fled to a nearby ally: Herod the Great.

Why Herod?

He's married to her half-sister. Here's where it gets confusing and potentially even grosser. Historical accounts describe Phraates V finding safety in Rome. Okay. Yet in the alternate version of the story, Herod offers her an estate for her and her young child. Child?!?! Remember, Phraates V is now about in his 20s AND in Rome. This child better not be under the age of six or...(vomit). The guy who wrote the Cleopatra thread into this vile story just stops the story here.

However...

"Let not the sin of his mother be blotted out"

Once again, Peter clearly establishes that Judas is the fulfillment of the Psalm 109 prophecy, and in the middle of the details, David brings up Judas's sinful mother. Yet Biblically, there is nada, zilch, nothing about any mother figure for Judas. Why would David sense evil a thousand years before the event happened? Why would David fixate on the "sins of a mother" unless it was majorly epic. Musa was real. Musa really married her son. Cleopatra's daughter is a theory. The incest baby is theory. Yet with all the Semiramis symbolism and connections to the Son of Perdition for Judas, she would be the perfect mother for Judas.

Too Far-fetched to Believe

So shortly after Judas hangs himself, his wife would learn the truth. What would she do? A common Hebrew might move to another town to avoid scandal, but Israel is pretty small. If the theory is true, Judas has the blood of Cleopatra, Julius Caesar, and Phraates (IV or V) in his veins. That's clout. Yet it's not safe to stay in Israel. So they travel to **"desolate places"** in southern France.

Instead of Mary Magdalene and Sarah landing at Saintes-Maries-de-la-Mer, it is Mrs. Iscariot and Sarah. Remember, the Gypsies and locals in Saintes-Maries-de-la-Mer celebrate the arrival of Sarah the Black. Sarah has a darker complexion (Egyptian/Roman/Parthian) than the mother (Hebrew). The father was somebody very, very important (just not Jesus). Do you dare say Judas Junior? Of course not. A devious lie and secret, like being the daughter of Jesus, could help keep the secret under wraps. If folks learned it was the bloodline of Judas? No help. If folks thought it was the secret bloodline of Jesus? "Hey

Jesus is cool, and keeping it a secret would protect the Church from a demystifying scandal."

How did it connect to the Gypsies?

No clue.

But it would be a great place to hide the bloodline, since they are "**continually vagabonds.**"

How does it connect to the Freemasons?

Well, according to all that Dan Brown lore, the French Merovingian kings claimed a divine bloodline. Their mythology? According to the Seventh Century *Chronicle of Fredegar*:

> **"It is said that while Chlodio was staying at the seaside with his wife one summer, his wife went into the sea at midday to bathe, and a beast of Neptune rather like a Quinotaur found her. In the event she was made pregnant, either by the beast or by her husband, and she gave birth to a son called Merovech, from whom the kings of the Franks have subsequently been called Merovingians."**

Recap: Beast from Sea. Really? Regardless of the mythological origins, Merovingians were strange, long-haired healers with supposed divine origins. Oh, and from the same region in France as Judas Junior. While they ruled for a while, the Catholic Church apparently ended the rule by sending assassins to take them out. The surviving heirs had "**their name be blotted out**" from the historical records after that, but right before the Crusades, a French nobleman with a secretive past is supported by mysterious enclave. The Frenchman? Godfrey of Bouillon. Historically, he joins the Crusades and becomes the first ruler of Jerusalem after the Holy Land is taken. This is where the Templar Knights fuse into the story. Historically, the Templar Knights lasted for another two centuries before the Catholic

Church once again takes them out. After that, the conspiracy theorists connect the remnants of the Templar Knights to re-birth in modern Freemasonry. Modern Freemasons don't like this connection, but the 20th Century's #1 Conspiracy Theory Nut (not Dan Brown) sure liked theories like this. It helps explain Hitler's motives.

And if Hitler did indeed fail?

Here comes the End Times…

Just as Jesus said, Judas had a connection as a Son of Perdi-tion. Just as Perdition (in theory) promised Judas two-thousand years ago, in exchange for betraying Jesus, his wife and children will be protected. Just as David predicted, the bloodline of curs-ed fathers and a wicked mother would continue for generation after generation. Just as Paul wrote, the truth about the Man of Sin would be revealed just before the End Times.

So when the Beast from Earth stands behind his main man the Antichrist, remember that this "Prophet of Evil" won't just be some regular Joe. He'll likely be a regular Judas.

ABOUT THE AUTHOR

Jason Lee Willis, a self-described Luth-olic-a-tist, characterizes himself as "just a nerd with a Bible" and has led adult and youth small group studies at home and at church for the past three decades. As a former English teacher who explored literature to find possibilities rather than absolute answers, Willis looks for "out of the box" interpretations with a preference for the most "epic" answers. While versed in world mythology and history, he remains the son of the church secretary raised in a conservative small town.

ALSO BY JASON LEE WILLIS
Examining the Beloved Disciple
Examining Moses
Examining Christmas
Examining Gospel Timelines